Editor
Mary S. Jones, M.A.

Editor in Chief
Karen J. Goldfluss, M.S. Ed.

Cover Artist
Barb Lorseyedi

Imaging
James Edward Grace
Craig Gunnell

Publisher
Mary D. Smith, M.S. Ed.

TCR 2939

Teacher Created Resources

101 Activities
for *Fast Finishers*

Grade 4

Keep kids engaged once their work is done!

Includes language arts, math, and critical thinking activities.

Great resource for busy teachers and quick-to-finish students!

Teacher Created Resources

Teacher Created Resources
6421 Industry Way
Westminster, CA 92683
www.teachercreated.com

ISBN: 978-1-4206-2939-2

© 2011 Teacher Created Resources
Made in U.S.A.

Teacher Created Resources

TABLE OF CONTENTS

INTRODUCTION

All students work at different speeds. Many take about the same amount of time to finish their work. Some are slower than others, and some are faster than others. You've probably been asked, "I'm done, what do I do now?" more times than you can count. But what's a teacher to do when one or more students finish early? The activity pages in *101 Activities for Fast Finishers* are the answer.

The 101 activities in this book focus on language arts, math, and critical thinking, and are divided as follows:

- Lively Language Arts (35 activities)
- Mind-Bender Math (35 activities)
- Beyond Brainy (31 activities)

Each activity has been labeled with an approximate amount of time that it will take students to complete. The estimated times range from 5 to 15 minutes. It is recommended that you copy, in advance, several pages representing the different times, and have them on hand to distribute, as needed. When a student asks you that famous "What do I do now?" question, a quick look at the clock will tell you which activity to give him or her. These activities will also be helpful to keep in your emergency substitute file as filler activities.

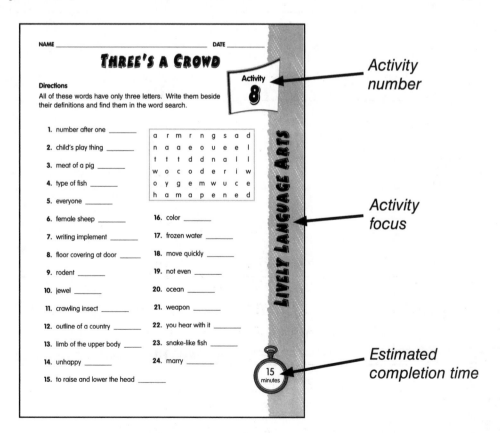

"ONE" MAKE

Activity 1

Directions

Make 14 words by adding a letter or group of letters to the word "one." Add the letter or letters to the beginning, the end, or both.

Example: someONE

1. _____

2. _____

3. _____

4. _____

5. _____

6. _____

7. _____

8. _____

9. _____

10. _____

11. _____

12. _____

13. _____

14. _____

LIVELY LANGUAGE ARTS

5 minutes

SAME LETTERS

Activity
2

Directions

Two words in each line have exactly the same letters in them.
Find and circle them.

1.	ant	ate	sea	tea	set
2.	flow	hold	wall	wolf	ball
3.	want	pant	wish	wasp	paws
4.	lump	bump	limp	pest	plum
5.	lame	lime	meal	make	sale
6.	bake	tame	meat	lake	take
7.	tail	mail	fail	lair	rail
8.	read	dare	care	bead	feed
9.	said	dine	edit	head	tide
10.	bleat	label	table	stables	chest
11.	care	pace	race	mace	fare
12.	stare	star	mare	rats	hats

5
minutes

ADDING LETTERS

Activity
3

Directions

Add one letter to each of the words below to make a word that fits the definition. The letter may be added to any part of the word.

Example: ban   farm building = barn

1. **and**   a body part   _____

2. **cot**   piece of clothing   _____

3. **fog**   animal that hops   _____

4. **net**   a bird's home   _____

5. **pin**   type of tree   _____

6. **sip**   a large boat   _____

7. **car**   a mark on the skin   _____

8. **bit**   used to catch fish   _____

9. **read**   food   _____

10. **stars**   steps   _____

5 minutes

TIMED WORDS

Activity
4

Directions

For each box below, set a timer for five minutes. See how many words you can write that contain "oo." Write these words in the top box. In the bottom box, see how many words you can write that contain "ee."

"oo" Words _____ _____ _____

_____ _____ _____ _____

_____ _____ _____ _____

_____ _____ _____ _____

_____ _____ _____ _____

_____ _____ _____ _____

"ee" Words _____ _____ _____

_____ _____ _____ _____

_____ _____ _____ _____

_____ _____ _____ _____

_____ _____ _____ _____

10 minutes

MAGIC LETTER SQUARES

Activity
5

Directions

Unscramble the letters beside each clue. Write the answer across the squares. When you have finished, you will find the same words also run downwards!

1. water container → (tnka) →

2. boy's name → (lAna) →

3. what people call you → (mnae) →

4. leg joint → (nkee) →

5. to mix with a spoon → (tsir) →

6. movements of ocean → (dtie) →

7. thought, notion → (eida) →

8. harvest, mow → (prae) →

9. better than all → (tesb) →

10. every one of seperate items → (heac) →

11. a mark on the skin → (crsa) →

12. drive-___ for fast food → (ruth) →

10 minutes

LIVELY LANGUAGE ARTS

FIND THE ADJECTIVES

Activity 6

Directions

There are 24 adjectives in this list of 40 words below.
Circle them first, and then find them in the word search.

```
G  L  I  L  L  X  F  F  B  R  R  Y  A  H  H
P  E  U  V  G  R  L  E  I  A  E  E  T  U  S
O  U  U  F  O  H  A  I  I  F  E  H  G  B  E
P  V  R  Z  R  U  W  L  N  U  T  E  E  K  R
U  N  E  P  T  O  I  G  N  X  I  E  T  G  F
L  N  Y  I  L  M  L  H  P  E  R  F  E  C  T
A  Y  F  H  A  E  A  O  L  H  O  Q  H  N  F
R  U  N  F  T  P  T  S  C  S  V  T  O  G  L
L  T  K  N  P  L  U  F  N  I  A  P  N  L  A
F  Z  H  Y  U  O  A  I  K  L  F  I  E  V  T
H  D  L  I  I  F  L  E  S  O  J  L  S  U  W
L  Y  P  R  N  C  H  W  H  O  M  P  T  O  G
A  D  E  U  N  A  E  L  C  F  T  I  G  H  T
F  S  H  U  N  G  R  Y  D  J  K  C  G  T  G
Y  R  Q  T  L  U  C  I  F  F  I  D  J  J  L
```

LIVELY LANGUAGE ARTS

ATTENTION	FAVOR	GRADUALLY	PAINFUL	SHOULDER
BEAUTIFUL	FAVORITE	HABIT	PERFECT	THIN
BLIZZARD	FIFTEEN	HEALTHY	PERFORM	THINK
CLEAN	FLAT	HONEST	POPULAR	TIGHT
COLORFUL	FOOLISH	HUGE	PARACHUTE	UMBRELLA
CURIOSITY	FRESH	HUNGRY	PURPLE	UNHAPPY
DIFFICULT	FROZEN	LAUGHTER	REPRESENT	WAGON
FAMILIAR	FUNNY	LEAP	SERIOUS	ZOO

15 minutes

WORD ROAD

Activity 7

Directions

How many words can you find in this word road without rearranging the letters?

t o g e t h e r a t e n o t e a m e

_____   _____

_____   _____

_____   _____

_____   _____

_____   _____

_____   _____

_____   _____

_____   _____

_____   _____

LIVELY LANGUAGE ARTS

5 minutes

THREE'S A CROWD

Activity 8

Directions

All of these words have only three letters. Write them beside their definitions and find them in the word search.

1. number after one _____

2. child's play thing _____

3. meat of a pig _____

4. type of fish _____

5. everyone _____

6. female sheep _____

7. writing implement _____

8. floor covering at door _____

9. rodent _____

10. jewel _____

11. crawling insect _____

12. outline of a country _____

13. limb of the upper body _____

14. unhappy _____

15. to raise and lower the head _____

16. color _____

17. frozen water _____

18. move quickly _____

19. not even _____

20. ocean _____

21. weapon _____

22. you hear with it _____

23. snake-like fish _____

24. marry _____

a	r	m	r	n	g	s	a	d
n	a	a	e	o	u	e	e	l
t	t	t	d	d	n	a	l	l
w	o	c	o	d	e	r	i	w
o	y	g	e	m	w	u	c	e
h	a	m	a	p	e	n	e	d

LIVELY LANGUAGE ARTS

15 minutes

PARTS OF SPEECH

Activity
9

Directions

Categorize the words in the box into six categories.
Place each word under the correct category.

jump	book	they	opened
he	found	gorgeous	loudly
thick	green	so	glasses
forcefully	happily	and	but
it	flew	George Washington	yet
heavy	she	sleepily	mother

Nouns	**Verbs**	**Pronouns**
_____	_____	_____
_____	_____	_____
_____	_____	_____
_____	_____	_____

Conjunctions	**Adverbs**	**Adjectives**
_____	_____	_____
_____	_____	_____
_____	_____	_____
_____	_____	_____

15
minutes

Write a sentence using one word from each category. _____

_____

SAME AND DIFFERENT

Activity 10

Directions

Look at the word in capital letters at the beginning of each row. Then circle the word in the row that has a similar meaning, and underline the word that has the opposite meaning.

1. **DIFFICULT** — hard   easy   cold   poor

2. **BROAD** — narrow   sweet   silly   wide

3. **START** — end   blue   sore   begin

4. **FALL** — drop   rise   stub   shoot

5. **WET** — old   damp   dry   sill

6. **DANGER** — garden   peril   safety   full

7. **UNHAPPY** — cheery   bent   sad   open

8. **LOFTY** — tall   old   short   delicate

9. **LISTEN** — fall   play   hear   talk

10. **FEEBLE** — strong   jolly   weak   new

10 minutes

LIVELY LANGUAGE ARTS

ANTONYMS

Activity
11

Directions

An antonym is an opposite. Fill in the puzzle with antonyms of the clues below.

LIVELY LANGUAGE ARTS

Across

- **2.** answer
- **3.** full
- **10.** modern
- **12.** easy
- **13.** hero
- **15.** guilty
- **16.** top

Down

- **1.** forget
- **4.** student
- **5.** here
- **6.** forward
- **7.** slow
- **8.** release
- **9.** crooked
- **11.** married
- **14.** tame

10 minutes

MAKING WORDS

Activity
12

Directions

How many words can you make by using the letters of the word *Constantinople*? Each word must have at least four letters. Each letter may only be used in any word the number of times it is used in *Constantinople*. For example, a word could not contain "pp" as there is only one "p" in *Constantinople*.

C O N S T A N T I N O P L E

_____   _____   _____

_____   _____   _____

_____   _____   _____

_____   _____   _____

_____   _____   _____

_____   _____   _____

_____   _____   _____

_____   _____   _____

_____   _____   _____

LIVELY LANGUAGE ARTS

10
minutes

TWOS

Directions

Start with the first letter, write it down in column 1, and then add every second letter and you will find a word to match part of the clue. Now start at the second letter and do the same thing in column 2 and you'll find another word that belongs with the first word.

LIVELY LANGUAGE ARTS

			Column 1	Column 2
1.	fbleye	two insects	_____	_____
2.	zteibgrear	two striped animals	_____	_____
3.	cnhoisne	two parts of the face	_____	_____
4.	tcahbalier	two pieces of furniture	_____	_____
5.	seeivgehnt	two numbers	_____	_____
6.	wmhoeteolr	two parts of a car	_____	_____

10 minutes

ONE TWO THREE

Activity

14

Directions

The words below have one, two, or three syllables. Count the syllables in each word and write them in the correct column.

laugh	bases	tacks
tickle	famous	goldfish
celebrate	brisk	air
furniture	neighborhood	telescope
runway	umbrella	city
ill	butterfly	cereal
impatient	reply	Earth
graph	month	canvas

One Syllable	Two Syllables	Three Syllables

LIVELY LANGUAGE ARTS

10
minutes

ODD ONE OUT

Activity

15

Directions

The three letters on each block make a word.
In each row of blocks, circle the one that is out of
place. Give your reasons.

1.

My reason: _____

2.

My reason: _____

3.

My reason: _____

4.

My reason: _____

5.

My reason: _____

LIVELY LANGUAGE ARTS

10 minutes

PAST TENSE

Directions

Think about forming the past tense to each of these words in the box. Then write each one in its past tense form in the correct column below.

equip	develop	prepare	slip	nod
arrive	happen	decide	rub	laugh
snap	finish	require	pass	raise

Just Add "d"	Double Final Consonant Add "ed"	Add "ed"

LIVELY LANGUAGE ARTS

5 minutes

THE LETTER E

Activity 17

Directions

Use the clues to fill in the blanks in the following words. All the words begin and end with the letter e. Then in the box below, rewrite the words in alphabetical order.

1. e __ __ __ __ __ e   to carry out

2. e __ __ __ e   the national bird

3. e __ __ __ __ e   to breathe out

4. e __ __ __ __ __ __ __ e   used to send a letter

5. e __ __ __ __ e   to get away

6. e __ __ __ __ __ __ __ __ e   to instill confidence

7. e __ __ __ __ __ __ __ e   to make a guess

8. e __ __ __ __ e   to tempt

9. e __ e   a female sheep

10. e __ __ __ __ __ __ e   to clear out

Alphabetical Order

a. _____   f. _____

b. _____   g. _____

c. _____   h. _____

d. _____   i. _____

e. _____   j. _____

15 minutes

LIVELY LANGUAGE ARTS

FUNNY PLURALS

Activity
18

Directions

Complete each joke by filling in the unusual plural for each noun in parentheses.

1. Why are _____ so well educated? (fish)

   . . . They live in schools.

2. What has three _____ but can't stand? (foot)

   . . . a yardstick

3. What gets the biggest laugh from the _____ who enjoy it the least? (person)

   . . . being tickled

4. What has _____ but never eats? (tooth)

   . . . a zipper

5. What is it that little _____ spend a lot of time making, yet no one ever sees? (child)

   . . . noise

6. How are _____ like icicles? (goose)

   . . . They both grow down.

7. Boy: "This morning my uncle shot two _____ in his pajamas." (deer)

   Girl: "How did the _____ get into your uncle's pajamas?" (deer)

8. How did _____ make wooden tools? (caveman)

   . . . a whittle at a time

9. What _____ make the best bookkeepers? (woman)

   . . . The ones who never return the books you lent them.

10. Boy: "Have you ever seen the Catskill Mountains?"

    Girl: "No, but I've seen them kill _____." (mouse)

5 minutes

LIVELY LANGUAGE ARTS

STARTERS

Activity 19

Directions

On the lines below, write the words that match the definitions. Each word begins with one of the letters in the box. Cross out this letter in the box after you have used it. With the leftover letters, find a monkey and a vegetable.

LIVELY LANGUAGE ARTS

```
a  t  b  c  l  k  s  e  m  i  p  d  e
```

1. animal with a hump _____

2. baby cat _____

3. insect that makes honey _____

4. large animal with a trunk _____

5. we get it from cows _____

6. number after 19 _____

7. animal that barks _____

8. the day after Friday _____

9. it has rungs and you climb up it _____

10. frozen water _____

5 minutes

monkey = _____   vegetable = _____

22

DICTIONARY DAZZLE

Activity 20

Directions

Use your dictionary (if needed) to help you add the missing word to these definitions. Then write the new words in alphabetical order below.

1. apricot — a small, orange colored _____

2. wasp — a kind of stinging _____

3. penguin — a black and white colored _____

4. panther — an animal that belongs in the _____

5. foal — a baby _____

6. sardine — a kind of small _____

7. bacon — meat that comes from a _____

8. harp — a musical instrument that has _____

9. wealthy — to have lots of _____

10. unicycle — a vehicle with one _____

Alphabetical Order

a. _____   f. _____

b. _____   g. _____

c. _____   h. _____

d. _____   i. _____

e. _____   j. _____

10 minutes

JOIN UPS

Directions

Make new words by joining the letter(s) at the end of Word 1 to the letter(s) at the beginning of Word 2. Use the clues to help you. An example has been done for you.

	Word 1	Word 2	Clue	Answer
	ro**be**	**ar**ts	animal	bear
1.	noon	ions	vegetable	
2.	lemon	keyboard	animal	
3.	ring	older	precious metal	
4.	acre	among	dairy food	
5.	grasp	arrows	bird	
6.	came	attack	flesh of animals	
7.	spin	kennels	color	
8.	stab	letters	furniture	
9.	skit	tender	young cat	
10.	glad	derive	climbing frame	

5
minutes

LIVELY LANGUAGE ARTS

ANALOGIES

Directions

Analogies are comparisons. Complete each analogy below.
An example has been done for you.

Wide is to narrow as tall is to short.

1. Big is to _____ as large is to small.

2. Hat is to head as shoe is to _____.

3. Bird is to nest as _____ is to hive.

4. Rug is to _____ as curtain is to window.

5. _____ is to road as boat is to lake.

6. Boy is to man as _____ is to woman.

7. _____ is to room as gate is to yard.

8. Sleep is to tired as _____ is to hungry.

9. Zoo is to animals as library is to _____.

10. Floor is to _____ as ceiling is to top.

11. _____ is to grass as blue is to sky.

12. Belt is to _____ as bracelet is to wrist.

13. Car is to driver as airplane is to _____.

14. Book is to _____ as television is to watch.

15. Grape is to vine as peach is to _____.

16. Ear is to hearing as _____ is to sight.

17. _____ is to day as dusk is to dawn.

18. Thanksgiving is to November as Christmas is to _____.

19. Calf is to cow as _____ is to lion.

20. _____ is to uncle as niece is to aunt.

LIVELY LANGUAGE ARTS

15 minutes

WORD LOOK

Activity 23

Directions

Look at the words in the box, and then answer the questions below.

| rainbow | write | eleven | thorough | cauliflower |

LIVELY LANGUAGE ARTS

1. Which word contains all the vowels? _____

2. Which word is made up of two smaller words? _____

3. Which word has an "i" as its middle letter? _____

4. Which word has only one vowel that is used three times? _____

5. Which of the words would come first in a dictionary? _____

6. Which of the words would come last in a dictionary? _____

7. Which word begins with two consonants and ends with two

   consonants? _____

8. Which word has eight letters? _____

9. Which word has the most consonants? _____

5 minutes

HOMOPHONE HUNT

Activity
24

LIVELY LANGUAGE ARTS

Directions

Above each sentence are two homophones. Choose the one that is needed to make the sentence correct. Write your answer on the line. The first one has been done for you.

1. **bear** or **bare**
   After the leaves fell, the tree looked _____bare_____ .

2. **doe** or **dough**
   The _____ wandered into the meadow with the other deer.

3. **hire** or **higher**
   Mr. Smith said he would _____ the boy to make deliveries.

4. **knot** or **not**
   She tied a _____ around the tree to hold the rope in place.

5. **maid** or **made**
   The hotel had a _____ come in every day to make the beds.

6. **mane** or **main**
   She braided the horse's _____ before the parade.

7. **peace** or **piece**
   A feeling of _____ settled over the valley at night.

8. **pain** or **pane**
   The ball crashed right through the window _____.

9. **soar** or **sore**
   They watched the eagle _____ through the air.

10. **tale** or **tail**
    The teacher read a _____ about a tortoise and a hare.

11. **tide** or **tied**
    Once each day, the _____ covers the sand with water.

12. **burro** or **burrow**
    The rabbit dove into its _____ quickly.

13. **creak** or **creek**
    The door made a loud _____ as it opened.

10 minutes

SMALL WORDS

Activity
25

Directions

Find a small word within the larger word in the box to complete each sentence. The first one has been done for you.

1. | stable | Mom put the knife on the _____table_____.

2. | shamble | She ate a _____ sandwich for lunch.

3. | problem | Be careful the thief does not _____ you!

4. | pajamas | I spread some strawberry _____ on the bread.

5. | obedient | Sam went to _____ at nine o'clock.

6. | garbage | Tina put all the carrots in the _____.

7. | height | I will be _____ years old tomorrow.

8. | furniture | The lady brushed my cat's smooth _____.

9. | haunt | My favorite _____ is visiting us next week.

10. | hundred | We painted the walls a bright _____.

11. | spangle | I cooked the scrambled eggs in a _____.

LIVELY LANGUAGE ARTS

5
minutes

TABLE WORDS

Activity
26

Directions

In the table below, write words that begin with the letters in the top row. The words must contain the number of letters indicated at the side of the table. Some words have been placed for you.

LIVELY LANGUAGE ARTS

	m	o	a	n	s
2	me				
3		one			
4				nest	
5					
6					starve

10
minutes

WORKING WITH ADVERBS

LIVELY LANGUAGE ARTS

Directions

Someone has written the wrong adverbs in the sentences below. Can you help correct them? Cross out the wrong word and write the correct adverb on the line. Then in the box below, join the sentence parts together to form sentences that make sense.

1. The horse ran slowly and won the race. _____

2. Jamie spoke softly, and everyone heard her. _____

3. We will go mountain bike riding yesterday. _____

4. The man went up the ladder to the ground. _____

5. A compass needle points south. _____

6. He crept	hard	for many days
7. I spoke	early	up the stairs.
8. He pushed	silently	so everyone could hear.
9. She arrived	north	and the door opened.
10. It rained	loudly	from Miami.
11. They traveled	heavily	and had to wait.

10 minutes

COMPOUND WORDS

Activity 28

Directions

Choose a word from Box A and combine it with a word from Box B to make a compound word. Some words will go together in more than one combination, but there is only one combination that will use all the words.

Box A

any-	south-
school-	back-
sea-	snow-
grand-	who-
home-	head-
under-	cow-
every-	news-
black-	bed-
rail-	after-
else-	out-

Box B

-road	-ball
-ever	-board
-shore	-east
-day	-paper
-made	-where
-doors	-boy
-one	-bone
-room	-stand
-father	-time
-noon	-line

_____   _____

_____   _____

_____   _____

_____   _____

_____   _____

_____   _____

_____   _____

_____   _____

_____   _____

_____   _____

15 minutes

LIVELY LANGUAGE ARTS

DOUBLE COMPOUND WORDS

LIVELY LANGUAGE ARTS

Directions

Write a word in the blank between each set of words. The trick is that the new word must complete a compound word both to the left and to the right of it. The first one has been done for you.

1. dug _____ out _____ side

2. foot _____ ladder

3. arrow _____ line

4. country _____ walk

5. tea _____ belly

6. camp _____ place

7. basket _____ room

8. touch _____ stairs

9. drug _____ keeper

10. base _____ room

11. flash _____ house

12. hill _____ walk

13. look _____ doors

14. quarter _____ bone

15. some _____ ever

10 minutes

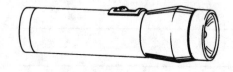

LANGUAGE ARTS TRIVIA

Activity
30

Directions

Answer each language arts trivia question below.

1. What are the two main parts of a sentence? _____

2. What punctuation mark is used in a contraction? _____

3. What word names a person, place, thing, or idea? _____

4. What do we call stories that are made up rather than true?

_____

5. In an address, what punctuation mark comes between the city and

state? _____

6. What do we call a statement that tells what a person thinks or

believes? _____

7. In a friendly letter, what punctuation mark is placed after the

greeting? _____

8. Give the contraction for *will not*. _____

9. What is the mini-dictionary in the back of some textbooks called?

_____

10. What is the plural of sheep? _____

11. In the dictionary, which comes first, *maybe* or *maypole*? _____

12. Do antonyms mean the same as or opposite of one another?

_____

10 minutes

TONE

Directions

Read each group of sentences below. Then write the tone each group of sentences expresses. Use each word only once.

happy	excited	funny	worried	sad

1. Wow! Today is my birthday. I know it will be a great day. We are having a chocolate cake, and we are going to play games. I can hardly wait until all my friends arrive to help me celebrate my special day.

Tone: _____

2. I can't believe my best friend is moving away. I want to cry. Even the sky looks gray and rainy today. Nothing will ever be the same again without my friend to share things with.

Tone: _____

3. Can a pig learn tricks? My pet pig, Sally, can roll over and shake hands. Maybe I should say she can shake pig's feet. She is a funny pig who really likes to "hog the show."

Tone: _____

4. I cannot believe that our math test is today. I forgot to study, and I do not understand multiplication. I just know I will fail this test. This could ruin my math grade. Oh, why didn't I study last night?

Tone: _____

5. It is an absolutely beautiful day today! The sun is shining, the birds are singing, and the air smells sweet and fresh. It feels good to be alive!

Tone: _____

10 minutes

UNDERSTANDING QUESTIONS

Activity 32

Directions

Read each question. Circle the type of answer you would give for each question. The first one has been done for you.

1. Who will help me go shopping for snacks for next week?

   (a. person)   b. place   c. yes/no   d. number   e. thing

2. Will you be able to watch TV with Robbie and me after school?

   a. person   b. place   c. way   d. choice   e. yes/no

3. Where is the school holding its annual winter festival this year?

   a. person   b. place   c. type   d. number   e. thing

4. Why did Grandpa volunteer to run a booth at the fair?

   a. person   b. reason   c. type   d. choice   e. person

5. How many people do you think will come to James' surprise party?

   a. person   b. type   c. number   d. choice   e. way

6. How did Uncle Robert fix the broken pedal on the boy's bike?

   a. place   b. number   c. yes/no   d. thing   e. way

7. What time did you say you were going to make dinner for us?

   a. person   b. place   c. thing   d. number   e. time

8. Where did Eric put the dishes that we need for our family picnic?

   a. person   b. place   c. time   d. reason   e. thing

9. Why do you think Tara left the party so early last night?

   a. number   b. yes/no   c. reason   d. thing   e. place

10. Is Aunt Pam's birthday on April 19th?

   a. place   b. thing   c. yes/no   d. number   e. time

LIVELY LANGUAGE ARTS

10 minutes

EARLY TO RISE

LIVELY LANGUAGE ARTS

Directions

Read the passage, and then answer the questions that follow.

An old man and a boy lived in a hut. The old man had taken the young boy as an apprentice. He was a carpenter, and he trained the boy to make things out of wood. Each morning, they would get supplies in town. They used the supplies to make items to sell.

The old man knew that some day the boy would be left alone. He wanted to teach him all he could. He decided to send the boy to town for supplies all by himself.

The old man woke the boy up at 5:00 in the morning and sent him on his way. The boy came home with all of his supplies, but he was exhausted. The next morning, he woke the boy up at 5:00 and sent him to town. The boy came home again with all he needed. On the third morning, the old man woke him again at 5:00. The boy wondered why the old man was doing this.

The next morning, the old man did not wake the boy. The boy woke up on his own. He didn't wake up until 8:00 in the morning and he did not get to town until 9:00 a.m. By the time he got to town, there were no supplies left. The wood pile had been picked over. Saddened, the boy returned home with little. He realized the lesson that the old man had been trying to teach him.

1. What happened first?
   a. The boy went to town at 5:00 a.m.
   b. The boy went to town at 9:00 a.m.
   c. The boy is taught to carve wood.
   d. The boy returns home with little.

2. What is the lesson the old man was trying to teach him?
   a. A rolling stone gathers no moss.
   b. What goes around comes around.
   c. Practice makes perfect.
   d. The early bird gets the worm.

3. Which of the following statements is true?
   a. The old man worked the boy too hard.
   b. The boy learned to get up early to get the good supplies.
   c. The boy forgot the day he was to go to town.
   d. The boy did not like living with the old man.

15 minutes

LADYBUGS

Activity 34

Directions

Read the passage, and then answer the questions that follow.

Have you ever seen a small, red beetle with black dots on its back? These little creatures are called lady beetles or ladybugs. Ladybugs are harmless insects. They do not bite or sting humans. They do not harm plants or carry diseases, either. In fact, ladybugs are quite helpful. Farmers and gardeners both like to see them on their plants. Why is that? It is because of what ladybugs eat.

Aphids are tiny insects that are harmful to many plants. Aphids suck the juices from plant leaves. This causes the leaves to shrivel up and die. Ladybugs have large appetites, and their favorite food is aphids. A ladybug can eat as many as 50 of them in a single day. For this reason, some people actually buy ladybugs at their garden store and set them free in their gardens.

Another advantage to having ladybugs in your garden is that you do not have to use insect poison to kill aphids. Many people, especially those growing fruits and vegetables, do not want to use poison on their plants. Letting ladybugs keep the number of aphids down is a natural way to grow healthy plants.

So if you happen to see a ladybug in a park or a garden, make sure to remember how helpful it can be. It might save your favorite plant one day!

1. The author says that ladybugs are harmless to humans. Which sentence supports that statement?
   a. Ladybugs have large appetites.
   b. Ladybugs are red with black spots.
   c. Ladybugs do not bite or sting.
   d. Ladybugs are found all across the U.S.

2. Why would some people not want to put insect poison on fruit and vegetable plants?
   a. They do not want to kill aphids.
   b. They do not want poison on their food.
   c. They do not know where to buy poison.
   d. They worry that the plants will die.

3. How does the passage compare aphids to ladybugs?
   a. Aphids are more destructive to a garden than ladybugs.
   b. Aphids are prettier than ladybugs.
   c. Aphids are more colorful than ladybugs.
   d. Aphids are hungrier than ladybugs.

15 minutes

LIVELY LANGUAGE ARTS

PANCAKE BREAKFAST

Activity **35**

Directions

Read the recipe and the story. Use them to answer the questions below.

Pancakes

Stir together:
  1 egg
  2 Tablespoons oil
  1 ¼ cup buttermilk

Sift together:
  1 ¼ cup flour
  1 teaspoon sugar
  1 teaspoon baking powder
  ½ teaspoon baking soda
  ½ teaspoon salt

Stir into liquid. Stir to blend all ingredients.

Heat 1 Tablespoon oil on griddle at 350°. Use a spoon to pour batter on pan to make a pancake.

Ben wanted to surprise his mother and make breakfast for her. He decided to cook pancakes.

Ben found an easy pancake recipe. His older sister helped him get out ingredients. She got the griddle and plugged it in.

Ben read the recipe and mixed the liquid ingredients in a large bowl. He added the dry ingredients and sifted them together. His sister helped him pour the batter on the griddle.

Ben cooked the pancakes until they were golden brown. He served them with melted butter and syrup. He brought the pancakes to his mother. She enjoyed her surprise.

1. Ben cooked the pancakes on a griddle. He used
  a. a barbecue.
  b. a large, flat pan with a handle.
  c. a long fork.
  d. a microwave.

2. The recipe calls for the same amount of which two ingredients?
  a. eggs and oil
  b. sugar and baking powder
  c. flour and salt
  d. buttermilk and eggs

3. Which ingredients did Ben mix first?
  a. ingredients that are sweet
  b. ingredients that are dry
  c. ingredients that are liquid
  d. ingredients that are salty

LIVELY LANGUAGE ARTS

15 minutes

BIG AND SMALL

Activity
36

Directions

Which truck in each row has the biggest load? For each truck, solve the math problems and add their answers together. Color the truck with the biggest total in each row. One truck has been done for you.

1.

a.
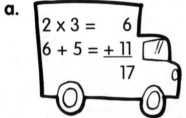

$2 \times 3 = 6$
$6 + 5 = \underline{+ 11}$
$ 17$

b.

$8 + 6 =$
$4 \times 3 =$

c.
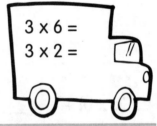

$3 \times 6 =$
$3 \times 2 =$

2.

a.
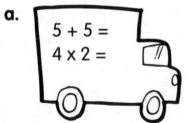

$5 + 5 =$
$4 \times 2 =$

b.

$5 \times 3 =$
$2 \times 5 =$

c.

$9 \times 2 =$
$1 \times 12 =$

3.

a.
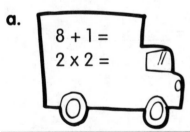

$8 + 1 =$
$2 \times 2 =$

b.

$9 + 5 =$
$6 \times 2 =$

c.

$3 \times 3 =$
$2 \times 6 =$

4.

a.

$5 \times 4 =$
$3 \times 3 =$

b.

$2 \times 5 =$
$4 \times 5 =$

c.

$6 + 7 =$
$3 \times 3 =$

10 minutes

NUMBERS FOR LETTERS

Activity 37

Directions

Solve the answers to the equations using the code below.

a = 2	b = 5	c = 3

1. a + b + c = _____

2. (a x b) + c = _____

3. (b + c) ÷ a = _____

4. a x b x c = _____

5. a + b – c = _____

6. a + (b x c) = _____

7. (b + c) – a = _____

8. (a x b) – c = _____

9. (a x c) – b = _____

10. (a + b) x c = _____

11. b + b + b + b = _____

12. b + b + c + c + a + a = _____

10 minutes

MIND-BENDER MATH

MISSING NUMBERS

Activity
38

Directions

Add the missing numbers in the squares to complete each number sentence.

1. $(2 \times 4) + \boxed{} = 10$

2. $10 - \boxed{} - 4 = 4$

3. $4 + 8 + \boxed{} = 16$

4. $(3 \times \boxed{}) + 4 = 13$

5. $(5 \times 3) - \boxed{} = 12$

6. $(10 \times \boxed{}) + 5 = 25$

7. $(20 \div 5) + \boxed{} = 8$

8. $16 - 3 - \boxed{} = 5$

9. $13 + \boxed{} + 5 = 20$

10. $20 - 10 - \boxed{} = 4$

11. $(16 \div \boxed{}) + 3 = 7$

12. $(5 \times \boxed{}) + 0 = 20$

MIND-BENDER MATH

5
minutes

WHAT'S THE TIME?

Activity
39

Directions

Write the times from the list below on the digital clocks. Then draw the hands showing the times on the analog clocks. The first one has been done for you.

MIND-BENDER MATH

1. twelve minutes past seven
2. six forty-four
3. ten twenty-five
4. six minutes before five

5. twenty-three minutes before three
6. eleven seventeen
7. two thirty-three
8. eighteen minutes after eight

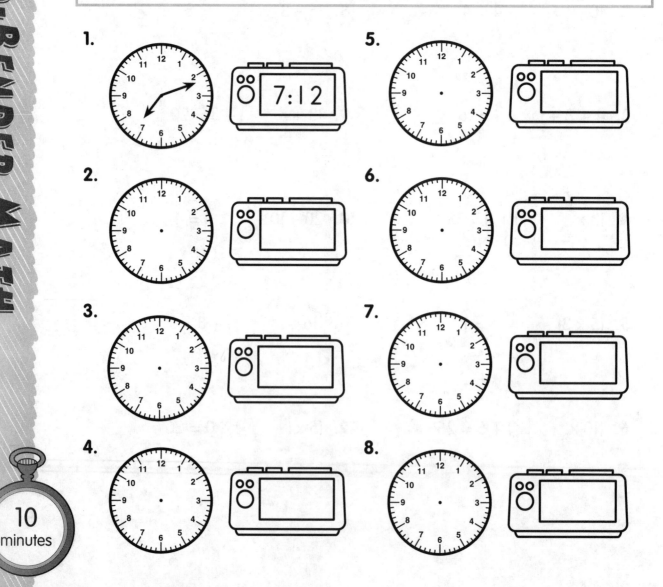

10 minutes

CUBES

Directions

How many small cubes are there in this shape?

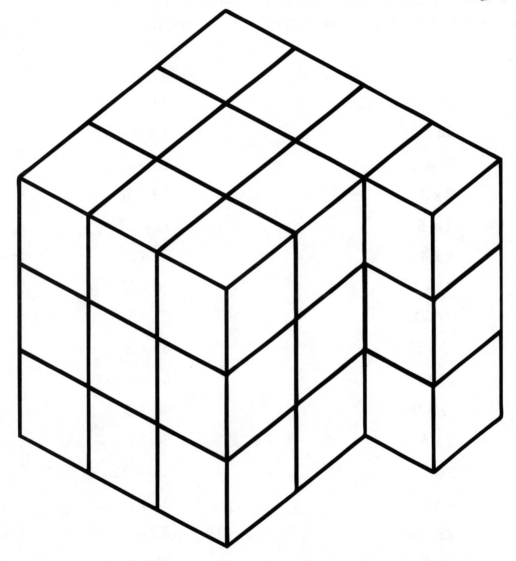

There are _____ small cubes.

5
minutes

ANSWER MATCH

Activity
41

MIND-BENDER MATH

Directions

Look at the left and right sides in the columns below. On each side, there are equations that have the same answer. Draw lines between equations that have the same answer. The first one has been done for you.

21 – 18	24 ÷ 12
44 – 36	9 ÷ 3
15 ÷ 3	28 ÷ 7
2 x 5	39 – 38
2 + 5	72 – 67
3 x 4	18 ÷ 3
34 ÷ 2	30 – 11
27 – 14	51 ÷ 3
17 – 15	35 ÷ 5
21 – 10	64 ÷ 8
19 – 18	60 ÷ 3
2 x 8	54 ÷ 6
2 x 7	120 ÷ 12
3 x 5	33 ÷ 3
22 – 16	2 x 6
3 x 3	15 + 3
5 x 4	52 ÷ 4
25 – 6	28 ÷ 2
6 x 3	36 – 21
16 ÷ 4	4 x 4

15 minutes

PRICE LISTS

Activity
42

Directions

If a = 5 cents, e = 10 cents, i = 15 cents, o = 20 cents,
u = 30 cents, and each consonant is worth 50 cents,
how much would each of the following groceries cost?

> **Example:** fruit = (f) 50¢ + (r) 50¢ + (u) 30¢ + (i) 15¢ + (t) 50¢ = $1.95

1. peach _____

2. salt _____

3. butter _____

4. milk _____

5. bread _____

6. flour _____

7. meat _____

8. sugar _____

MIND-BENDER MATH

10 minutes

MAGIC NUMBER SQUARES

Activity 43

Directions

A magic square is a set of numbers arranged in the form of a square so that the numbers in each row, each column, and each diagonal add up to the same total. Complete the following magic squares. You can use a number more than once. The number in the star indicates the total.

MIND-BENDER MATH

1. ★9

4		5
	3	
		2

4. ★12

7		1
		5

2.  ★12

		2
	4	
6	3	

5. ★9

1		
	2	5

3. ★9

1	6	2
4		

6. ★15

1		
6	7	

 10 minutes

NUMBER RELATIONS

Activity
44

Directions

Think about the relationship between the first two numbers. What number will make the last two numbers relate to each other in the same way? Circle the number and write it in the box.

MIND-BENDER MATH

1. 5 is to 10 as 4 is to [ ] .   3 8 4 2

2. 3 is to 5 as 7 is to [ ] .   6 5 0 9

3. 4 is to 7 as 3 is to [ ] .   3 6 9 5

4. 3 is to 8 as 5 is to [ ] .   7 10 12 6

5. 10 is to 20 as 8 is to [ ] .   14 16 12 9

6. 10 is to 7 as 6 is to [ ] .   4 3 8 5

5
minutes

HOW FAR?

Activity
45

Directions

These insects are on their way home. Use your ruler to measure the paths each has to make (in centimeters). Who has the farthest to go? Write the distances on the lines.

1.

distance: _____

2.

distance: _____

3.

distance: _____

10 minutes

Multiples Tree

Activity 46

Directions

Color all the multiples of 4 blue.
Color all the multiples of 5 red.
Color all the multiples of 7 green.

MIND-BENDER MATH

(16)

(15) (8)

(5) (14) (10)

(12) (4) (36) (45)

(21) (49) (7) (25) (32)

(91) (30) (24) (55) (42) (50)

(77) (48)

(88) (65)

(44) (63)

10 minutes

LETTERS AND NUMBERS

Activity 47

Directions

Under each letter in the box below is the number it represents. Use these letters and numbers to answer the questions that follow.

T	B	N	Y	U	P	E	O	I	A	D
5	10	3	7	6	1	4	9	8	2	0

1. Which number represents the fifth letter in the row?_____

2. What is the total of the numbers that represent the vowels? _____

3. What is the total of the numbers that represent the letters of the word BEAN? _____

4. What number represents the middle letter of the row?_____

5. Add up the total of the numbers that represent the consonants and take it away from the total of the numbers that represent the vowels.

   _____

6. What words are represented by each of these number groups?

   a. | 10 | 2 | 10 | 7 | _____

   b. | 1 | 2 | 8 | 0 | _____

   c. | 0 | 4 | 2 | 3 | _____

   d. | 5 | 9 | 2 | 0 | _____

MIND-BENDER MATH

10 minutes

SEESAW MATH

Directions

Find an expression from the box below that will balance each seesaw. Write the equivalent expression on the other end of the seesaw. You will not use all of the expressions. The first one has been done for you.

9 + 7	7 + 3 + 3	8 + 4 + 8	19 – 12	21 – 12	12 – 8
4 + 6 + 5	3 + 6 + 9	3 + 4 + 5	17 – 6	21 – 7	3 + 1 + 4

1. 15 – 8   19 – 12

2. 14 + 6

3. 17 – 8

4. 21 – 6

5. 18 – 5

6. 13 – 5

7. 3 + 8

8. 5 + 6 + 7

9. 14 – 7 – 3

10. 3 + 8 + 5

10
minutes

MIND-BENDER MATH

YELLOW OR GREEN?

Activity 49

Directions

Color all the boxes that equal 20 yellow.
Color all the boxes that equal 12 green.

MIND-BENDER MATH

1. 6 x 2 =	6. 16 + 4 =	11. 24 ÷ 2 =	16. 12 + 8 =
2. 40 ÷ 2 =	7. 7 + 5 =	12. 40 − 10 − 10 =	17. 5 x 4 =
3. 6 + 6 =	8. 18 − 6 =	13. 4 x 5 =	18. 24 − 6 − 6 =
4. 10 x 2 =	9. 20 − 8 =	14. 3 + 9 =	19. (6 x 3) − 6 =
5. 15 − 3 =	10. 18 + 2 =	15. 28 − 4 − 4 =	20. 11 + 9 =

5 minutes

TOTAL UP

Activity
50

Directions

Look at the numbers in the shapes, and then answer the questions below.

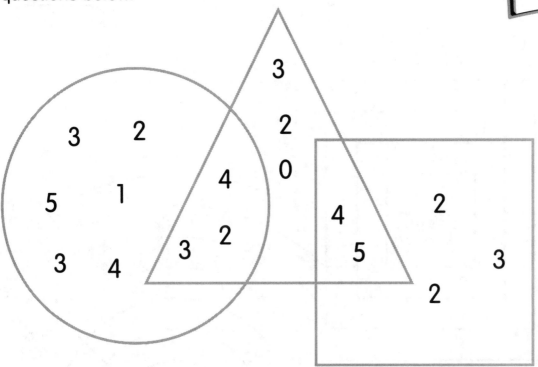

Mind-Bender Math

1. What is the total of the numbers in the square but not in any other shape? _____

2. What is the total of the numbers that are in both the circle and the triangle, but not in any other shape? _____

3. What is the total of the numbers in the triangle but not in any other shape? _____

4. What is the total of all the numbers in all the shapes? _____

5 minutes

NAME _____ DATE _____

PRIME NUMBERS

Directions

Follow the path of prime numbers to reach the end of the maze.

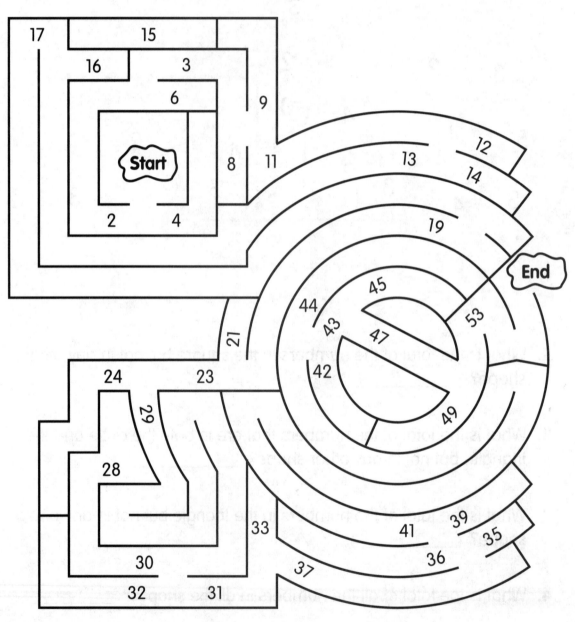

5 minutes

MIND-BENDER MATH

OPERATION BOXES

Activity
52

Directions

Fill in each blank space with a number so that everything that touches is true and positive.

1.

			=	6
=		+		−
6				7
−				=
4	=		+	

↓

3.

	+	4		5
=		=		=
6		8		1
−		−		−
			=	

↑

2.

	=		+	
	13		6	
	−		=	
=				−
5	+		=	9

↑

4.

7	=	4	−	
=				=
	+	3		
				+
	−	14	=	3

→

MIND-BENDER MATH

10 minutes

COSTLY SHAPES

Activity
53

Directions

Find the cost of each diagram below, according to the price list.

Price List

straight line = 10¢

empty circle = 20¢

black dot = 5¢

1.

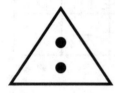 cost = _____

4.

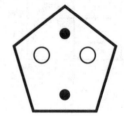 cost = _____

2.

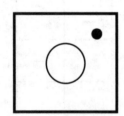 cost = _____

5.

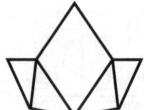 cost = _____

3.

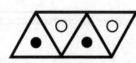 cost = _____

6.

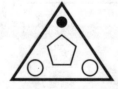 cost = _____

5
minutes

MIND-BENDER MATH

NAME _____ DATE _____

MATH CODES

Activity 54

Directions

Each number below is framed by a different shape. Using this as a guide, write the correct number in each shape below, and then solve each problem.

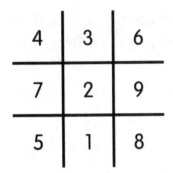 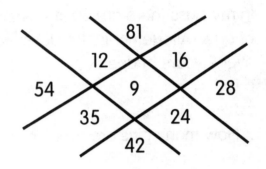

Example: (⌐8 ÷ □2) × (54> ÷ ◇9) = 4 × 6 = 24

1. (∧ ÷ └)   ×   (◇ ÷ ⊔) = _____

2. (⟩ ÷ ⌐)   ×   (∨ ÷ ⌐) = _____

3. (⟍ ÷ □)   ×   (< ÷ ⌐) = _____

4. (> ÷ ⌐)   ×   (< ÷ ⌐) = _____

5. (< ÷ ⌐)   ×   (◇ ÷ ⌐) = _____

15 minutes

©*Teacher Created Resources*   57   *#2939 101 Activities for Fast Finishers*

BOYS AND GIRLS

Activity
55

Directions

Read the text in the box, and then answer the
questions that follow.

> In my class there are 20 students and 12 of them are over 9 years
> of age. Altogether in the class there are 12 boys of whom 5 are
> over 9 years of age.

1. How many girls are over 9?   _____

2. How many girls are under 9?   _____

3. How many boys are over 9?   _____

4. How many boys are under 9?   _____

5. How many girls are there in the class?   _____

6. How many more boys than girls are
there in the class?   _____

5
minutes

TOUCHY NUMBERS

Activity
56

Directions

Fill in the blank boxes with the numbers 1–5. Each full row and column contains the numbers 1, 2, 3, 4, and 5. Each shaded number is the sum of all the numbers touching it.

1.

	3	2	1	
	25		25	5
1		3	4	2
3	24	1	22	
4		5	3	

2.

4	2		5	3
3	22		24	5
	2		1	
1	25		24	2
2	3		4	1

MIND-BENDER MATH

10 minutes

WHAT'S MISSING?

Activity 57

Directions

Complete each number sentence by writing in the missing factors on the lines below that would make both sides equal. Write each answer as a number word in the puzzle. See #1 Across. It has been done for you.

MIND-BENDER MATH

Across

1. $25 \times 2 = 10 \times$ ___5___
2. $6 \times 2 =$ _____ $\times 4$
4. $3 \times 14 =$ _____ $\times 6$
5. $4 \times 13 = 52 \times$ _____
8. $4 \times 20 =$ _____ $\times 5$
9. $8 \times 5 = 4 \times$ _____
11. $22 \times 2 = 1 \times$ _____
13. $15 \times 4 = 3 \times$ _____
15. $3 \times 8 =$ _____ $\times 6$
17. $1 \times 39 = 3 \times$ _____

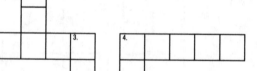

Down

1. $8 \times 8 = 16 \times$ _____
2. $5 \times 4 = 10 \times$ _____
3. $4 \times 4 =$ _____ $\times 2$
4. $14 \times 4 = 8 \times$ _____
6. $12 \times 6 =$ _____ $\times 8$
7. $10 \times 10 =$ _____ $\times 2$
10. $16 \times 3 = 4 \times$ _____
12. $28 \times 2 =$ _____ $\times 4$
14. $6 \times 6 = 4 \times$ _____
16. $10 \times 3 = 5 \times$ _____

15 minutes

RIGHT OR WRONG?

Directions

Color only those boxes that have the correct answers.

11 + 4 = 16	6 + 8 + 9 = 23	(3 x 2) + 9 = 15
12 – 7 = 3	20 – 3 – 6 = 11	19 – 6 = 14
4 + 8 + 3 = 15	20 ÷ 5 = 4	15 – 3 = 10
8 + 3 + 7 = 18	18 – 2 – 5 = 13	9 + 11 + 5 = 25
17 + 4 = 22	11 + 11 + 4 = 26	30 – 2 – 2 = 26
(10 x 2) + 10 = 30	99 + 2 = 104	3 x 2 x 2 = 12
(3 x 6) – 2 = 16	(10 ÷ 2) + 11 = 16	5 x 5 = 26
14 + 5 + 8 = 28	28 – 3 – 3 = 22	(10 x 10) + 10 = 110

MIND-BENDER MATH

5
minutes

NAME THAT MOVIE

Activity
59

MIND-BENDER MATH

Directions

In 1903, one of the first successful feature-length movies was produced. What was the name of that movie? To discover the answer, find the sum for each addition problem. Write the letter that matches each sum on the lines below.

1. 2,101 + 2,416	3. 4,943 + 8,123	5. 4,278 + 7,696	7. 9,101 + 9,456	9. 3,198 + 1,553	11. 4,772 + 8,323
A	**B**	**E**	**G**	**H**	**I**
2. 6,579 + 1,568	4. 2,937 + 3,797	6. 2,584 + 5,108	8. 1,081 + 1,654	10. 2,101 + 9,769	
N	**O**	**R**	**T**	**Y**	

___ ___ ___   ___ ___ ___ ___ ___
2,735 4,751 11,974   18,557 7,692 11,974 4,517 2,735

___ ___ ___ ___ ___
2,735 7,692 4,517 13,095 8,147

___ ___ ___ ___ ___ ___ ___
7,692 6,734 13,066 13,066 11,974 7,692 11,870

15 minutes

62

MULTIPLICATION SQUARES

Activity 60

Directions

Multiply going across and down. Write the missing numbers. An example has been done for you.

Example

× →		
5	5	25
6	2	12
30	10	300

Square #3

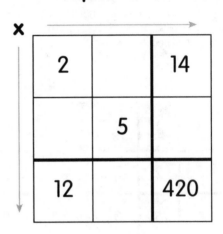

× →		
2		14
	5	
12		420

Square #1

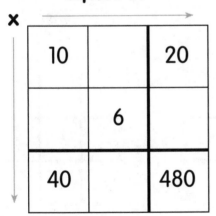

× →		
10		20
	6	
40		480

Square #4

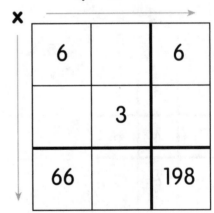

× →		
6		6
	3	
66		198

Square #2

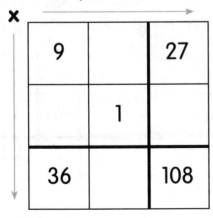

× →		
9		27
	1	
36		108

Square #5

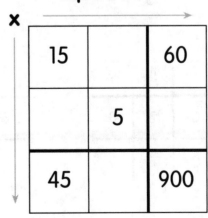

× →		
15		60
	5	
45		900

15 minutes

THREE IN A ROW

Activity
61

Directions

In each grid below, circle the three numbers in a row that equal the number in the gray circle when multiplied. The numbers can be in a vertical, horizontal, or diagonal line.

MIND-BENDER MATH

48

1.

3	1	9
6	2	7
4	5	8

120

4.

8	6	4
9	5	2
7	1	3

180

7.

1	3	8
7	6	2
4	5	9

42

2.

7	3	2
1	4	8
9	6	5

100

5.

4	9	5
7	3	5
0	2	4

108

8.

2	7	5
9	9	9
6	3	8

24

3.

2	4	6
0	2	8
2	7	9

72

6.

7	8	2
6	4	3
9	4	1

162

9.

6	3	7
2	6	4
8	9	8

15 minutes

SOLVE THE PUZZLE

Directions

Use the figure below and the following clues to solve this problem. Notice that each section of the figure is labeled with a letter. Find out what number goes in each section and what color it should be. Write your answers in the appropriate sections.

Clues:

- The number in the red section is twice as much as the number in the F section.

- The yellow section is five.

- The smallest number is in the blue section.

- The sum of the numbers in E and G is thirteen.

- The only prime number is in E.

MIND-BENDER MATH

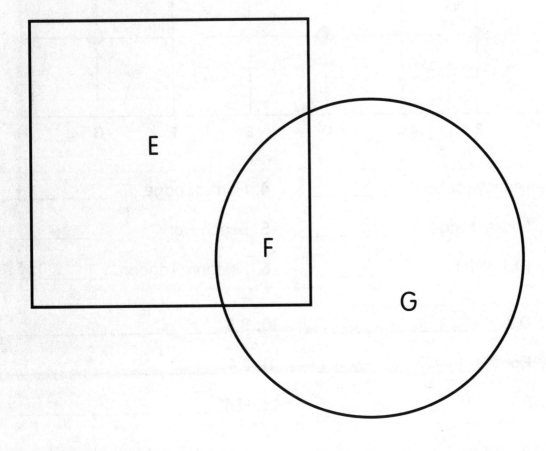

10 minutes

MAP COORDINATES

Activity

63

MIND-BENDER MATH

Directions

In the first box, give the position coordinates for the following locations on Emu Island. In the second box, name what is located at the given points.

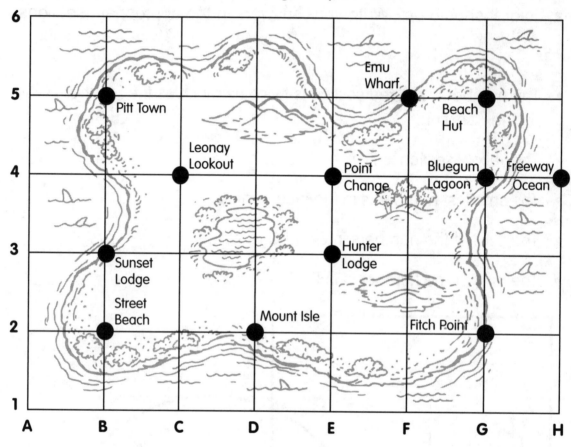

---

1. Leonay Lookout _____	**4.** Hunter Lodge _____
2. Sunset Lodge _____	**5.** Beach Hut _____
3. Fitch Point _____	**6.** Bluegum Lagoon _____

---

7. D,2 _____	**10.** B,5 _____
8. F,5 _____	**11.** E,4 _____
9. B,2 _____	**12.** H,4 _____

10 minutes

MATH VOCABULARY

Activity **64**

Directions

Look at the words in Column 1. On the line provided,
write the letter of its matching definition from Column 2.

Column 1	Column 2
_____ **1.** area	**A.** a line that is at a right angle to another line
_____ **2.** congruent	**B.** the answer to a subtraction problem
_____ **3.** difference	**C.** lines that run side by side that never cross and never meet
_____ **4.** equation	**D.** the answer to an addition problem
_____ **5.** parallel	**E.** equal in shape or size
_____ **6.** perimeter	**F.** the distance around the edge of a shape (side + side + side + side)
_____ **7.** perpendicular	**G.** a number sentence or statement
_____ **8.** product	**H.** the answer to a multiplication problem
_____ **9.** quotient	**I.** the amount of surface within a given boundary, measured in square units
_____ **10.** sum	**J.** the answer to a division problem

10 minutes

MYSTERY NUMBERS

Activity
65

Directions

Follow the clues to discover the mystery numbers.

75	31	35	10	36
41	84	86	53	22
49	99	88	18	17
27	93	46	94	11
24	29	57	52	31

558	346	891	626	324
191	310	223	594	628
777	818	125	813	899
412	541	946	311	715
461	837	675	576	241

1. Cross off all numbers that are the following:

- divisible by 9
- multiples of 5
- have two even digits
- have two odd digits
- have two digits that when multiplied together equal 36
- when one digit is subtracted from the other, the difference is 3

What is the mystery number?

_____

2. Cross off all numbers that are the following:

- contain all odd or all even digits
- have a 3 as one of the digits
- have a number larger than 5 in the tens place
- have a number smaller than 5 in the hundreds place
- divisible by 9
- even numbers

What is the mystery number?

_____

MIND-BENDER MATH

15 minutes

FUNNY FRACTIONS

Activity
66

Directions

A funny message is hidden below. To find it, find the fraction of the word in each problem below. As you find each fraction, write the letters in order on the lines at the bottom of the page. The first two have been done for you.

1. the first 1/3 of *ice*
2. the first 2/5 of *water*
3. the last 2/5 of *plant*
4. the last 2/3 of *bed*
5. the first 2/4 of *toad*
6. the last 3/4 of *gown*
7. the first 1/2 of *at*
8. the first 2/3 of *bat*
9. the first 2/3 of *key*
10. the last 2/4 of *very*

11. the first 3/6 of *butter*
12. the last 1/3 of *ski*
13. the first 3/5 of *count*
14. the last 2/4 of *cold*
15. the last 2/4 of *rant*
16. the first 4/6 of *raisin*
17. the last 1/2 of *me*
18. the first 3/4 of *them*
19. the first 2/3 of *dog*
20. the last 3/5 of *cough*

<u>I</u>   <u>W</u> <u>A</u> ___ ___ ___ ___   ___ ___   ___ ___ ___

___   ___ ___ ___ ___ ___ , ___ ___ ___

                    ,
___ ___ ___ ___ ___ ___ ___ ___   ___ ___ ___ ___

___ ___ ___ ___   ___ ___ ___ ___ .

10 minutes

DIVISION SQUARES

Activity
67

MIND-BENDER MATH

Directions

Divide going across and down. Write the missing numbers. An example has been done for you.

Example

÷

12	3	4
6	3	2
2	1	2

Square #1

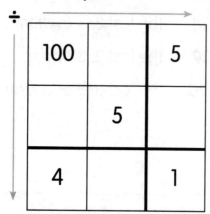

÷

100		5
	5	
4		1

Square #2

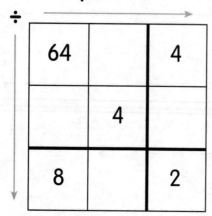

÷

64		4
	4	
8		2

Square #3

÷

30		5
	2	
3		1

Square #4

÷

16		2
	2	
4		1

Square #5

÷

120		3
	20	
2		1

15 minutes

NAME _____ DATE _____

MYSTERY MESSAGE DIVISION

Directions

The top boxes contain division problems, and the bottom boxes contain the answers. Solve each problem and find its answer in the bottom boxes. Then write the word from the problem box into the correct answer box. Your result will be a funny message. The first one has been done for you.

Problems

1. $6\overline{)198}$ — $\begin{array}{r}33\\-18\\\hline 18\\-18\\\hline 0\end{array}$ *who*	**4.** $4\overline{)5,627}$ *me*	**7.** $3\overline{)401}$ *said,*	**10.** $8\overline{)1,032}$ *the*
2. $5\overline{)8,971}$ *in*	**5.** $7\overline{)368}$ *weeder."*	**8.** $9\overline{)872}$ *Martians*	**11.** $2\overline{)3,074}$ *"Take*
3. $6\overline{)6,784}$ *your*	**6.** $4\overline{)819}$ *garden*	**9.** $3\overline{)9,070}$ *to*	**12.** $5\overline{)617}$ *landed*

Answers

96 r8	33 who	123 r2	1,794 r1
129	204 r3	133 r2	1,537
1,406 r3	3,023 r1	1,130 r4	52 r4

15 minutes

MATH TRIVIA

Activity

69

Directions

Answer each math trivia question below.

1. How many inches are in a yard? _____

2. How many weeks are in a year? _____

3. Turn 3/2 into a mixed fraction. _____

4. What is the denominator in the fraction 7/8? _____

5. What is the numerator in the fraction 5/9? _____

6. What do you call the answer to a multiplication problem? _____

7. Which of the following is not a prime number: 3, 5, 7, 9, 11? _____

8. What number comes next in this series: 1, 3, 6, 10, 15 . . . ? _____

9. What do you call a shape that has 8 sides? _____

10. What do you call the answer to a division problem? _____

11. What is 5 squared? _____

12. How many centimeters are in a meter? _____

13. How many nickels are in a dollar? _____

14. What is half of 30? _____

15. What do we find when we multiply the length times the width of a rectangle? _____

16. What is 3,489 rounded to the nearest hundred? _____

10 minutes

MIND-BENDER MATH

GEOMETRICALLY SPEAKING

Directions

Each section of the figure below is labeled with a letter. Your task is to find out which whole number goes in each section and what color it should be. Use the following clues to help you solve this problem. Write your answers in the appropriate sections.

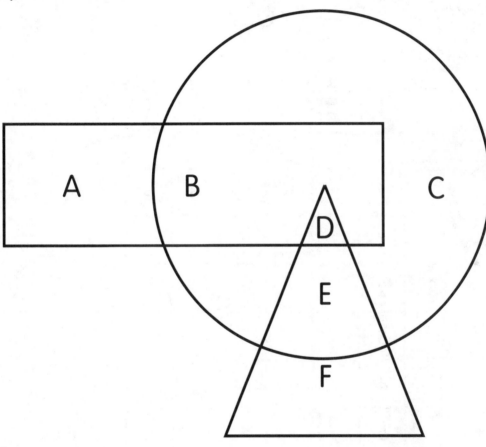

MIND-BENDER MATH

Clues:

- The sum of the triangle is 15.
- The section that is in all three shapes is colored green.
- The rectangle has the red, white, and green sections in it.
- The orange section is the number 8.
- The product of section D and the blue section is 21.

- The 5 section is purple.
- A is red.
- The sum of the rectangle is 11.
- E is blue.
- The sum of the circle is 20.
- The sum of A and B is 8.

15 minutes

PICTURE PUZZLE

Activity
71

Directions

Write the name of each object across each row in the grid below. Then using the numbers and letters in the grid, discover the words using the given grid coordinates to find the letters.

1.

2.

3.

4.

5.

	a	b	c	d	e
1					
2					
3					
4					
5					

6. 2a   2b   1d   3d   5e   _____

7. 5b   5d   1c   5a   4d   3e   _____

8. 1e   2c   5a   1b   _____

9. 2b   4b   4a   2c   _____

10. 3a   5d   3e   4e   2e   _____

10
minutes

BEYOND BRAINY

LOOK AND THINK

Activity

72

Directions

Look at the finished train puzzle below. Which group,
A, B, or C, includes all the pieces that make the full train
puzzle? Circle the correct letter.

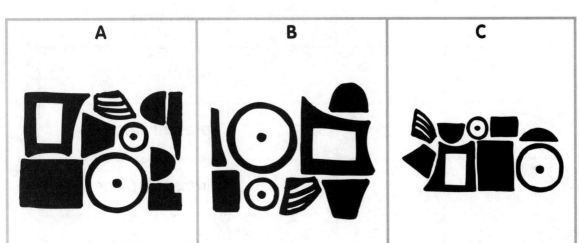

BEYOND BRAINY

5
minutes

FROM BEGINNING TO END

Activity
13

Directions

Can you turn the word "ADD" into "ZOO" in ten tries by changing one letter at a time? Use the clues to the right to help you.

BEYOND BRAINY

A	D	D	
			help or assist
			a cover
			started a flame
			lice egg
			a seed from a tree
			a fish trap
			not old
			present time
			transport a car
			also
Z	O	O	

5 minutes

HOLIDAYS

Activity 74

Directions

The following puzzle contains the names of 17 special days that are celebrated throughout the year from New Year's Day through Christmas. Can you find all 17?

```
H E Q S L A B O R D A Y G X F V N L
A M C H R I S T M A S F T W O I A I
L D V Z Y U M M L B L B K H U S P N
L W V E T E R A N S D A Y S R T R P
O E P M E M O R I A L D A Y T P I R
W A S L I N C T L N O I R T H A L E
E S N T B E F I N P E I H L O T F S
E T W F D A C N T G D D C E F R O I
N E N H R R A L W M C G E Y J I O D
I R E A U S O K I O A Z L K U C L E
K V A L E N T I N E S D A Y L K S N
M R Q C S C O N L L C L V D Y S D T
U T H A N K S G I V I N G H E D A S
M O T H E R S D A Y E U H S Y A Y D
O B N E W Y E A R S D A Y O F Y U A
B T K A U K O Y F A T H E R S D A Y
G J G F C O L U M B U S D A Y H Y O
```

Beyond Brainy

10 minutes

KATY'S NOTEBOOK

Directions

Katy lost her notebook. Can you help her find it?
Circle the correct notebook. Here are facts about
Katy's notebook:

✔ It has stripes and her name on the front.

✔ It is square.

✔ It does not have stars on it.

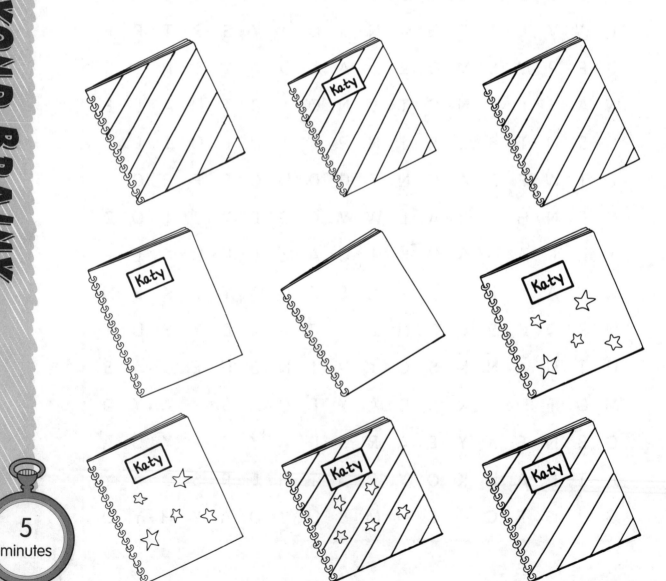

B E Y O N D   B R A I N Y

5 minutes

NAME _____ DATE _____

CREATURE CODES

Directions

Use the codes to figure out the names of the creatures below.

a	b	c	d	e	f	g	h	i	j	k	l	m
✻	◉	✳	❄	❆	❆	✳	✳	✳	✳	✳	●	○

n	o	p	q	r	s	t	u	v	w	x	y	z
■	❑	❐	❑	❑	▲	▼	◆	❖	◗	◇	▮	▮

1. ✳ ❑ ❐ ▲ ✳ _____

2. ✳ ❑ ■ ✳ ✳ ▮ _____

3. ▮ ✳ ◉ ❐ ✻ _____

4. ○ ❑ ◆ ▲ ✳ _____

5. ✳ ❑ ◉ ▼ _____

6. ▼ ✳ ✳ ✳ ❐ _____

7. ▲ ❐ ◉ ❐ ❐ ❑ ◗ _____

8. ❑ ❑ ◉ ✳ ■ _____

9. ✳ ◉ ✳ ● ✳ _____

10. ▲ ◗ ◉ ● ● ❑ ◗ _____

11. ❑ ✳ ■ ✳ ◆ ✳ ■ _____

12. ✳ ❑ ❐ ✳ ◉ ◉ ◆ ❐ ❑ ◉ _____

10 minutes

Jelly Bean Sudoku

Activity
11

Directions

Color every jelly bean with an indicated color.
No color can be repeated in a column, row, or box.

R = Red	**Y** = Yellow	**P** = Purple
RV = Red Violet	**G** = Green	**Pk** = Pink
O = Orange	**B** = Blue	**Bk** = Black

BEYOND BRAINY

Puzzle grid:

Row 1: B, O, _, _, _, G, P, _, Y
Row 2: P, R, Y, _, _, _, _, _, _
Row 3: G, _, Bk, _, R, _, O, _, B
Row 4: _, G, _, _, _, _, Bk, _, RV
Row 5: Bk, P, _, Y, _, RV, _, G, R
Row 6: RV, _, R, _, _, _, _, P, _
Row 7: R, _, B, _, O, _, RV, _, Pk
Row 8: _, _, _, _, _, _, R, O, G
Row 9: O, _, G, RV, _, _, _, Y, P

15
minutes

ABC Puzzlers

Directions

Each equation below contains the initials of words that will make the statement correct. Find the missing words. An example has been done for you.

> **Example:** 5 D in a ZC = 5 digits in a zip code

1. 26 L in the A _____

2. 52 W in a Y _____

3. TE invented the LB _____

4. a 4LC means GL _____

5. 52 C in a D of C _____

6. 4 Q in a D _____

7. 3 sides on a T, but 4 sides on a S _____

8. 7 C on planet E _____

9. an I has 6 L, but a S has 8 L _____

10. at 32 D, water F _____

11. GW was the first P _____

12. 360 D in a C _____

13. 64 S on a CB _____

14. 4 S on a V, but 6 S on a G _____

15. a U has 1 W, but a B has 2 W _____

Beyond Brainy

10 minutes

HIDDEN ANIMALS

Activity
79

Directions

Hidden in each sentence are three or four animal names. Can you find them? Circle them and write the names on the lines.

Example: Hel(p ig)loos! ➔ pig

1. My grandmother feels you should always capitalize Brandon.

_____

2. The coward, ogre, and boy ran hard and tried to grab bits of food.

_____

3. The bowl's crunchy enamel was enough to anger Bill.

_____

4. The scowling wizard's wands made the limo useless.

_____

5. The flea gleefully came late to the blob's term party.

_____

6. Common keywords to realize Brazil are rainfall, Amazon, and soccer.

_____

BEYOND BRAINY

10 minutes

CLIPPED WORDS

Directions

The following words are written in their shortened forms.
Write the long form of each word on the line to its right.

1. phone _____

2. champ _____

3. gas _____

4. vet _____

5. bike _____

6. plane _____

7. tux _____

8. math _____

9. ref _____

10. auto _____

11. fridge _____

12. sub _____

13. gym _____

14. taxi _____

15. burger _____

16. specs _____

17. limo _____

18. exam _____

BEYOND BRAINY

10 minutes

ODD ONE OUT

Activity 81

Directions

In each list below, circle the item that does not belong in the group and explain why on the line.

1. Gala, McIntosh, Bartlett, Red Delicious, Granny Smith

   _____

2. girl, niece, mom, sister, daughter-in-law, nephew, grandmother

   _____

3. January, March, November, October, December, August

   _____

4. cirrus, calculus, cumulus, stratus, cirrostratus, altocumulus

   _____

5. hexagon, octagon, oxygen, square, sphere, triangle, cube

   _____

6. centimeter, decimeter, kilometer, hectogram, kilogram, ounce, deciliter

   _____

7. red, yellow, blue, orange

   _____

8. factor, product, multiple, sum, multiply

   _____

9. dogwood, iris, rose, carnation, lily, tulip, orchid

   _____

10. rabbit, frog, toad, bunny, turtle, grasshopper, cricket

   _____

BEYOND BRAINY

15 minutes

DRAWING PATTERNS

Activity 82

Directions

Complete each of the shapes so that they match the first shape.

1.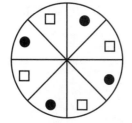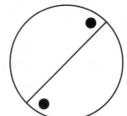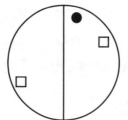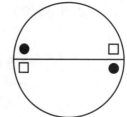

2.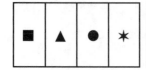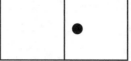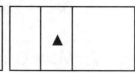

3.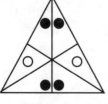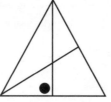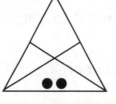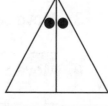

4.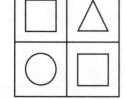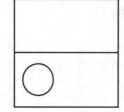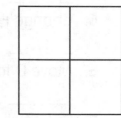

5.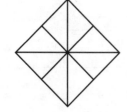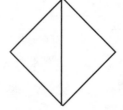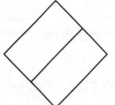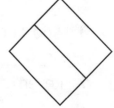

6.

BEYOND BRAINY

10 minutes

LETTER SCRAMBLE

Activity

8 3

Directions

Change the letters in the starting clue by following the directions below. When moving letters, the remaining letters will move over. When you finish, you will reveal the name of the U.S. president the clue refers to.

> **Starting Clue:** FIRST TO RIDE A TRAIN

1. Delete each I.

___ ___ ___ ___ ___ ___ ___ ___ ___ ___ ___ ___ ___ ___ ___

2. Move O in front of N.

___ ___ ___ ___ ___ ___ ___ ___ ___ ___ ___ ___ ___ ___ ___

3. Move second A to front.

___ ___ ___ ___ ___ ___ ___ ___ ___ ___ ___ ___ ___ ___ ___

4. Move S between R and O.

___ ___ ___ ___ ___ ___ ___ ___ ___ ___ ___ ___ ___ ___ ___

5. Change F to N.

___ ___ ___ ___ ___ ___ ___ ___ ___ ___ ___ ___ ___ ___ ___

6. Move D to the third position from the left.

___ ___ ___ ___ ___ ___ ___ ___ ___ ___ ___ ___ ___ ___ ___

7. Delete all Ts.

___ ___ ___ ___ ___ ___ ___ ___ ___ ___ ___ ___ ___

8. Add J in front of the second A.

___ ___ ___ ___ ___ ___ ___ ___ ___ ___ ___ ___ ___ ___

9. Reverse fifth and sixth letters.

___ ___ ___ ___ ___ ___ ___ ___ ___ ___ ___ ___ ___ ___

10. Delete the sixth letter.

___ ___ ___ ___ ___ ___ ___ ___ ___ ___ ___ ___ ___

11. Replace the eighth letter with CK.

___ ___ ___ ___ ___ ___ ___ ___ ___ ___ ___ ___ ___ ___

12. Add W in front of the J.

___ ___ ___ ___ ___ ___ ___ ___ ___ ___ ___ ___ ___ ___ ___

COUNTRY REBUS

Activity

8 4

Directions

Decode each rebus below, and write the country name.

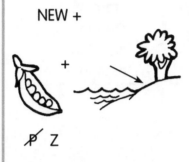

NEW +

1. _____

4. _____

7. _____

−H + S

2. _____

5. _____

8. _____

+ ADA

IS +

PURR

+ OO

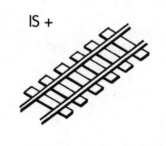

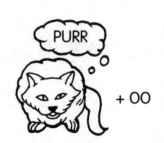

3. _____

6. _____

9. _____

10 minutes

BEYOND **B**RAINY

HIDDEN MEANINGS

Activity
85

Directions

Explain the hidden meaning of each box.

W A T E R	vitamins vitamins vitamins vitamins vitamins	vision vision

1. _____   4. _____   7. _____

le g	$\dfrac{vacation}{ccccc}$	ssssssssssse

2. _____   5. _____   8. _____

CH**MADE**INA	BDSPELER	SDRAW

BEYOND BRAINY

10 minutes

3. _____   6. _____   9. _____

JIGSAW

Activity
86

Directions

Look at the pictures in the squares below. Draw them in the empty grid so they make a bird. Then color the finished picture.

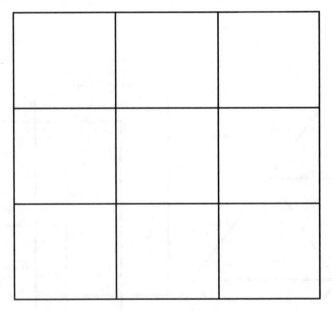

BEYOND BRAINY

10 minutes

TRIANGLES AND RECTANGLES

Directions

Count the number of triangles in the first shape.
Count the number of rectangles in the second shape.

BEYOND BRAINY

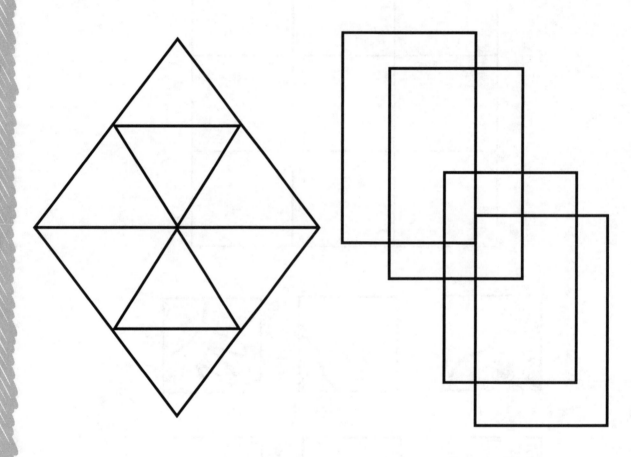

_____ triangles   _____ rectangles

10 minutes

NUMBER TRIVIA

Directions

Look at the numbers in the box below. Circle sets of three numbers that add up to eight. You can only circle each number once. When circling numbers you may not cross another line. You must use all of the numbers.

2	0	8	0	1
1	5	4	7	0
3	1	3	5	1
4	1	1	5	2
7	0	0	2	0
1	8	0	7	1

BEYOND BRAINY

10 minutes

GROWING LARGER

Activity
89

Directions

Look at the picture in the small grid. Using the squares to help you, draw it again in the larger grid below. Color your picture.

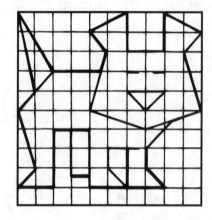

5 minutes

LICENSE PLATES

Activity
90

Directions

Many license plates are personalized with special messages. Can you decode the following license plates? The first one has been done for you.

1. | IMHOT |

   _____I'm hot_____

2. | IGO4IT |

   _____

3. | BLKVELVT |

   _____

4. | LOVENU |

   _____

5. | URNOZE |

   _____

6. | BURNRUBR |

   _____

7. | YRPL8HR |

   _____

8. | LDYBG |

   _____

9. | RSECRET |

   _____

10. | ANTQLVR |

    _____

11. | BBALSTR |

    _____

12. | IM2BZ |

    _____

BEYOND BRAINY

10 minutes

FUTURE JOBS

Activity

91

Directions

Miguel, Anna, Tran, and Lisa want to have different careers when they grow up. Read each clue.
Then mark the chart to see who wants which career.

Clues:

✔ Tran wants to be either a teacher or the President.

✔ Neither Miguel nor Anna wants to be a doctor.

✔ Miguel doesn't want to be a lawyer or the President.

		President	Doctor	Lawyer	Teacher
	Miguel				
	Anna				
	Tran				
	Lisa				

1. What does Miguel want to be? _____

2. What does Anna want to be? _____

3. What does Tran want to be? _____

10 minutes

4. What does Lisa want to be? _____

BEYOND BRAINY

WORD WINDERS

Activity

92

Directions

Use the clues to help you fill in the blanks and circles.
Only the circled letters change from one word to the next.

1. antonym for hot   <u>c</u>   <u>o</u>   <u>l</u>   <u>d</u>

2. pony

3. stroke of lightning

4. courageous

5. without hair

6. object used in a soccer game

7. device that rings

8. item worn around the waist

9. to soften by using heat

10. to shed skin

11. green, furry growth of fungi

12. small, burrowing animal

13. empty space

14. to hang on to something

15. yellow metallic element

16. to bend and crease

17. what you eat

18. one who lacks good sense

19. object used to do work

20. place to swim

BEYOND BRAINY

10 minutes

Fun with Idioms

Activity 93

Directions

Fill in the blanks with the words in the word bank to complete the idioms. Then use the missing words to complete the crossword puzzle. 3 Down has been done for you.

uptake
ends
cake
draw
gas
trigger
bee
log
beaver
colors
out

Across

2. Burn yourself _____ — to overwork yourself and become exhausted

4. Piece of _____ — an easy and pleasant task

6. Quick on the _____ — ready, alert, and quick to respond

8. Busy as a _____ — working hard and at a steady pace

10. With flying _____ — with ease and success

Down

1. Cooking with _____ — performing with skill and getting the job done

3. Quick on the ___uptake___ — ready, alert, and quick to respond

5. Burn the candle at both _____ — to overwork yourself and become exhausted

7. Quick on the _____ — ready, alert, and quick to respond

8. Busy as a _____ — working hard and at a steady pace

9. Easy as rolling off a _____ — very easy

10 minutes

SHAPE CODE

Activity
94

Directions

Use the letter code in the shapes below to discover the
hidden messages. Write the final messages on the lines.

s	t	i	n	e	b	h	a
c	m	v	r	d	w	o	u

1.

_____

2.

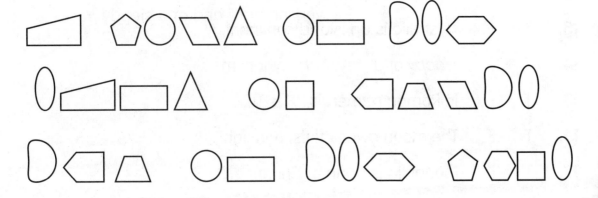

10
minutes

Beyond Brainy

TRUE OR FALSE

**Activity
95**

Directions

Before each of the following statements, circle T if the statement is true and F if the statement is false. If the statement is false, correct it so that it is true.

BEYOND BRAINY

1. T   F   Thanksgiving comes before Labor Day.

2. T   F   A telescope is used to view things that are far away.

3. T   F   Thirty-three times twenty-seven is an even number.

4. T   F   The Pacific Ocean is on the east coast of North America.

5. T   F   A hexagon has fewer sides than an octagon.

6. T   F   A baby goat is called a kid.

7. T   F   The color red is a primary color.

8. T   F   Jefferson was the fourth president of the United States.

9. T   F   Eight hours past 5:00 p.m. is 1:00 a.m.

10. T   F   The Washington Monument is in the state of Washington.

11. T   F   Abraham Lincoln is pictured on a quarter.

12. T   F   All insects have six legs.

13. T   F   Australia is an island continent.

14. T   F   *Happy* and *merry* are synonyms.

15. T   F   In Roman numerals, IX is 11.

16. T   F   The moon gives off its own light.

17. T   F   Mongolia is north of China.

18. T   F   The fourteenth letter of the alphabet is "M."

**10
minutes**

GEOGRAPHY CLUES

Activity
96

Directions

Figure out the geography clues below and find your answers in the word search. Use the words from the box to help you.

VOLCANO	AUSTRALIA	OCEANS	SOUTH POLE
CALIFORNIA	FRANCE	MOUNTAINS	EARTHQUAKE
EQUATOR	JUNGLE	HAWAII	LAKE

```
S  H  R  Q  P  W  X  I  A  M  T  R
F  O  G  O  D  N  I  Q  O  J  W  M
S  J  U  G  T  A  M  U  P  E  N  E
S  S  Q  T  W  A  N  F  K  Q  A  C
O  Y  N  A  H  T  U  A  R  H  U  N
V  N  H  A  A  P  U  Q  Y  T  S  A
W  O  E  I  E  Q  O  L  E  A  T  R
O  A  N  A  H  C  P  L  D  Q  R  F
Y  S  A  T  N  N  O  T  E  L  A  L
X  T  R  O  N  A  C  L  O  V  L  A
C  A  L  I  F  O  R  N  I  A  I  K
E  T  L  C  J  U  N  G  L  E  A  E
```

Beyond Brainy

1. This is a mountain that "blows its top."

2. It is extremely cold in this place.

3. When the ground starts shaking, it could be this.

4. This country's capital is Paris.

5. These are the world's largest bodies of water.

6. This U.S. state is the farthest west.

7. You might find a koala here.

8. You climb a long time to reach the top of these.

9. This place has thick vegetation and wild animals.

10. This body of water is good for swimming and boating.

11. Many movies are made in this West Coast U.S. state.

12. This is an imaginary line around the center of the globe.

15 minutes

MIXED-UP RIDDLES

Activity 97

Directions

Can you solve these riddles? Think carefully before you write.

1. As soon as it's spoken, it's broken. What is it?

2. What runs up and down the stairs without moving?

3. What gets wetter and wetter the more it dries?

4. I'm lighter than a feather and yet the strongest person has trouble holding me for more than a minute. What am I?

5. I move and jump, copying your exact movements, but I never see you. What am I?

6. In me, *yesterday* follows *today*, and *tomorrow* is somewhere in between. What am I?

7. I'm locked up tight. The only way to get me out is by breaking me. What am I?

8. I can be seen, but I weigh nothing. Put me in a bucket or pail and I will make it a lighter load. What am I?

9. What runs, but can't walk? What has a mouth, but never talks? What has a bed, but never goes to sleep?

10. I can be thrown off a tall building and I won't break. I can be thrown into a car, and still I won't break. But, if you throw me in a river or the ocean, I will slowly break into pieces. What am I?

10 minutes

BEYOND BRAINY

PRESIDENTIAL FACTS

Activity
98

Directions

In each of the puzzles below, each letter of the alphabet stands for another letter. You must break the code to answer each of the riddles. All of the answers will be the names of U.S. presidents. Part of the code is given below.

Z = A	V = E	R = I	L = O	F = U

1. This president had two women attempt to assassinate him in the same month!

____ ____ ____ ____ ____ ____   ____ ____ ____ ____
T   V   I   Z   O   W   U   L   I   W

2. He was the oldest man elected president.

____ ____ ____ ____ ____ ____   ____ ____ ____ ____ ____ ____
I   L   M   Z   O   W   I   V   Z   T   Z   M

3. He lived most of his life with a bullet two inches away from his heart.

____ ____ ____ ____ ____ ____   ____ ____ ____ ____ ____ ____ ____
Z   M   W   I   V   D   Q   Z   X   P   H   L   M

4. This president had to borrow money to go to his own inauguration.

____ ____ ____ ____ ____ ____   ____ ____ ____ ____ ____ ____ ____ ____ ____ ____
T   V   L   I   T   V   D   Z   H   S   R   M   T   G   L   M

5. He was the first president to live in the White House.

____ ____ ____ ____   ____ ____ ____ ____ ____
Q   L   S   M   Z   W   Z   N   H

6. He was shot in Ford's Theater.

____ ____ ____ ____ ____ ____ ____   ____ ____ ____ ____ ____ ____ ____
Z   Y   I   Z   S   Z   N   O   R   M   X   L   O   M

7. This president had the most children. He had 15!

____ ____ ____ ____   ____ ____ ____ ____ ____ ____
Q   L   S   M   G   B   O   V   I

15
minutes

ABSORB TO ZEBRA

Activity

99

Directions

Write a word that begins with "A" and ends with "B." Continue through the alphabet. Finish with a word that starts with "Z" and ends with "A." The list has been started for you. (**Note:** You may not find a word for every letter combination.)

a _____ absorb _____ b   n _____ o

b _____ basic _____ c   o _____ p

c _____ d   p _____ q

d _____ e   q _____ r

e _____ f   r _____ s

f _____ g   s _____ t

g _____ h   t _____ u

h _____ i   u _____ v

i _____ j   v _____ w

j _____ k   w _____ x

k _____ l   x _____ y

l _____ m   y _____ z

m _____ n   z _____ a

BEYOND BRAINY

15 minutes

OLYMPIC SPORTS RIDDLES

Activity
100

Directions

Read the clues and use the sports from the box to fill in the blanks. Use the numbered letters to fill in the blanks below and complete the puzzle.

archery	gymnastics	rowing	wrestling	fencing
luge	cycling	equestrian	skating	

1. This sport is sometimes used for hunting.

__ __ __ __ __ __ __
1   9

2. This freestyle sport was once popular at the ancient Olympic Games.

__ __ __ __ __ __ __ __ __
  2

3. College teams often compete in this water sport.

__ __ __ __ __ __
3

4. Men and women perform acrobatic tumbling movements.

__ __ __ __ __ __ __ __ __ __
4   7

5. The foil, epee, and saber are used in the sport.

__ __ __ __ __ __ __
  5

6. The slider wears a tight rubber suit and pointed boots. __ __ __ __
        8

7. Show jumping and dressage are events in this sport.

__ __ __ __ __ __ __ __ __ __
10   6

8. Riders race in a large group called a *peloton*.

__ __ __ __ __ __ __
11

9. Having good blades is important in all events of this sport.

__ __ __ __ __ __ __
12

Beyond Brainy

The site of the first modern Olympic Games:
City: __ __ __ __ __ __   **Country:** __ __ __ __ __ __ __
  1 7 9 2 6 12   4 3 10 5 11 8

10 minutes

PHONE CODES

Directions

Use the letters on the phone keypad to help you solve the phone code puzzles below.

BEYOND BRAINY

1. Iris' phone number is **736-4846**. If someone asks her for her number, Iris gives the name of an animal instead of telling the digits. Which animal does she name?

   ____ ____ ____ ____ ____ ____ ____

2. Gladys' phone number is **222-2243**. If someone asks her for her number, Gladys gives the name of a vegetable instead of telling the digits. Which vegetable does she name?

   ____ ____ ____ ____ ____ ____ ____

3. Matt's phone number is **486-4279**. If someone asks him for his number, Matt gives the name of a country instead of telling the digits. Which country does he name?

   ____ ____ ____ ____ ____ ____ ____

4. Ivan's phone number is **887-5474**. If someone asks him for his number, Ivan gives the name of a language instead of telling the digits. Which language does he name?

15 minutes

   ____ ____ ____ ____ ____ ____ ____

Answer Key

Activity 1
Answers will vary.
Possible answers include:
bone, cone, done, gone, lone, none, tone, zone, phone, shone, stone, alone, etc.

Activity 2
1. ate, tea
2. flow, wolf
3. wasp, paws
4. lump, plum
5. lame, meal
6. tame, meat
7. lair, rail
8. read, dare
9. edit, tide
10. bleat, table
11. care, race
12. star, rats

Activity 3
1. hand
2. coat
3. frog
4. nest
5. pine
6. ship
7. scar
8. bait
9. bread
10. stairs

Activity 4
Answers will vary.

Activity 5
1. tank
2. Alan
3. name
4. knee
5. stir
6. tide
7. idea
8. reap
9. best
10. each
11. scar
12. thru

Activity 6
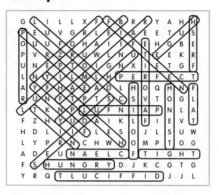

Activity 7
together, to, get, the, era, a, ether, her, rat, at, rate, ate, ten, no, not, note, tea, team, am, me, he

Activity 8
1. two
2. toy
3. ham
4. cod
5. all
6. ewe
7. pen
8. mat
9. rat
10. gem
11. ant
12. map
13. arm
14. sad
15. nod
16. red
17. ice
18. run
19. odd
20. sea
21. gun
22. ear
23. eel
24. wed

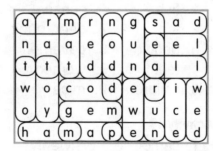

Activity 9
Nouns: book, George Washington, glasses, mother
Verbs: jump, found, flew, opened
Pronouns: he, it, she, they
Conjunctions: so, and, but, yet
Adverbs: forcefully, happily, sleepily, loudly
Adjectives: thick, heavy, green, gorgeous

Activity 10
1. circled: hard
   underlined: easy
2. circled: wide
   underlined: narrow
3. circled: begin
   underlined: end
4. circled: drop
   underlined: rise
5. circled: damp
   underlined: dry
6. circled: peril
   underlined: safety
7. circled: sad
   underlined: cheery
8. circled: tall
   underlined: short
9. circled: hear
   underlined: talk
10. circled: weak
    underlined: strong

Activity 11
Across
2. question
3. empty
10. ancient
12. difficult
13. villain
15. innocent
16. bottom

ANSWER KEY (cont.)

Activity 11 (cont.)
Down
1. remember   8. capture
4. teacher   9. straight
5. there   11. single
6. backward   14. wild
7. quick

Activity 12
Answers will vary. Possible answers include: acts, ants, cans, cattle, clans, cleats, clone, coast, coats, east, last, lion, list, lost, nest, nine, none, nose, ones, pact, paint, pants, past, patent, pest, pine, plant, plot, pole, post, saint, scan, scant, spine, spot, stain, stop, slip, snip, taint, talent, tans, taps, tips, tons, tops, etc.

Activity 13
1. fly, bee
2. zebra, tiger
3. chin, nose
4. table, chair
5. seven, eight
6. wheel, motor

Activity 14
One Syllable: laugh, ill, graph, brisk, month, tacks, air, Earth
Two Syllables: tickle, runway, bases, famous, reply, goldfish, city, canvas
Three Syllables: celebrate, furniture, impatient, neighborhood, umbrella, butterfly, telescope, cereal

Activity 15
1. pen; others are animals
2. yam; others are clothing
3. rib; others are numbers
4. cup; others are insects
5. sat; others are foods

Activity 16
Just Add "d": arrived, prepared, decided, required, raised
Double Final Consonant: equipped, snapped, slipped, rubbed, nodded
Add "ed": developed, happened, finished, passed, laughed

Activity 17
1. execute   a. eagle
2. eagle   b. encourage
3. exhale   c. entice
4. envelope   d. envelope
5. escape   e. escape
6. encourage   f. estimate
7. estimate   g. evacuate
8. entice   h. ewe
9. ewe   i. execute
10. evacuate   j. exhale

Activity 18
1. fish   6. geese
2. feet   7. deer, deer
3. people   8. cavemen
4. teeth   9. women
5. children 10. mice

Activity 19
1. camel   6. twenty
2. kitten   7. dog
3. bee   8. Saturday
4. elephant 9. ladder
5. milk   10. ice
monkey = ape
vegetable = pea

Activity 20
1. fruit   a. bird
2. insect   b. fish
3. bird   c. fruit
4. jungle   d. horse
5. horse   e. insect
6. fish   f. jungle
7. pig   g. money
8. strings   h. pig
9. money   i. strings
10. wheel   j. wheel

Activity 21
1. onion   6. meat
2. monkey   7. pink
3. gold   8. table
4. cream   9. kitten
5. sparrow 10. ladder

Activity 22
1. little   11. Green
2. foot   12. waist
3. bee   13. pilot
4. floor   14. read
5. Car   15. tree
6. girl   16. eye
7. Door   17. Night
8. eat   18. December
9. books   19. cub
10. bottom   20. Nephew

Activity 23
1. cauliflower
2. rainbow
3. write
4. eleven
5. cauliflower
6. write
7. thorough
8. thorough
9. cauliflower

Answer Key (cont.)

Activity 24
1. bare
2. doe
3. hire
4. knot
5. maid
6. mane
7. peace
8. pane
9. soar
10. tale
11. tide
12. burrow
13. creak

Activity 25
1. table
2. ham
3. rob
4. jam
5. bed
6. bag
7. eight
8. fur
9. aunt
10. red
11. pan

Activity 26
Answers will vary.

Activity 27
1. change slowly to quickly
2. change softly to loudly
3. change yesterday to tomorrow
4. change up to down
5. change south to north
6. He crept silently up the stairs.
7. I spoke loudly so everyone could hear.
8. He pushed hard and the door opened.
9. She arrived early and had to wait.
10. It rained heavily for many days.
11. They traveled north from Miami.

Activity 28
anyone, schoolroom, seashore, grandfather, homemade, understand, everyday, blackboard, railroad, elsewhere, southeast, backbone, snowball, whoever, headline, cowboy, newspaper, bedtime, afternoon, outdoors

Activity 29
1. out
2. step
3. head
4. side
5. pot
6. fire
7. ball
8. down
9. store
10. ball
11. light
12. side
13. out
14. back
15. where

Activity 30
1. subject, predicate
2. apostrophe
3. noun
4. fiction
5. comma
6. opinion
7. comma
8. won't
9. glossary
10. sheep
11. maybe
12. opposite of

Activity 31
1. excited
2. sad
3. funny
4. worried
5. happy

Activity 32
1. a
2. e
3. b
4. b
5. c
6. e
7. e
8. b
9. c
10. c

Activity 33
1. c
2. d
3. b

Activity 34
1. c
2. b
3. a

Activity 35
1. b
2. b
3. c

Activity 36
1. a. 17, b. 26, c. 24
2. a. 18, b. 25, c. 30
3. a. 13, b. 26, c. 21
4. a. 29, b. 30, c. 22

Activity 37
1. 10
2. 13
3. 4
4. 30
5. 4
6. 17
7. 6
8. 7
9. 1
10. 21
11. 20
12. 20

Activity 38
1. 2
2. 2
3. 4
4. 3
5. 3
6. 2
7. 4
8. 8
9. 2
10. 6
11. 4
12. 4

ANSWER KEY (cont.)

Activity 39
1. 7:12   5. 2:37
2. 6:44   6. 11:17
3. 10:25   7. 2:33
4. 4:54   8. 8:18

Activity 40
There are 30 small cubes.

Activity 41
21 – 18 = 9 ÷ 3
44 – 36 = 64 ÷ 8
15 ÷ 3 = 72 – 67
2 x 5 = 120 ÷ 12
2 + 5 = 35 ÷ 5
3 x 4 = 2 x 6
34 ÷ 2 = 51 ÷ 3
27 – 14 = 52 ÷ 4
17 – 15 = 24 ÷ 12
21 – 10 = 33 ÷ 3
19 – 18 = 39 – 38
2 x 8 = 4 x 4
2 x 7 = 28 ÷ 2
3 x 5 = 36 – 21
22 – 16 = 18 ÷ 3
3 x 3 = 54 ÷ 6
5 x 4 = 60 ÷ 3
25 – 6 = 30 – 11
6 x 3 = 15 + 3
16 ÷ 4 = 28 ÷ 7

Activity 42
1. $1.65   5. $1.65
2. $1.55   6. $2.00
3. $2.40   7. $1.15
4. $1.65   8. $1.85

Activity 43

1.
4	0	5
4	3	2
1	6	2

4.
3	3	6
7	4	1
2	5	5

2.
5	5	2
1	4	7
6	3	3

5.
1	4	4
6	3	0
2	2	5

3.
1	6	2
4	3	2
4	0	5

6.
8	3	4
1	5	9
6	7	2

Activity 44
1. 8   4. 10
2. 9   5. 16
3. 6   6. 3

Activity 45
1. ant = 14 ½ cm
2. ladybug = 14 cm
3. worm = 14 cm

Activity 46
Blue: 16, 8, 12, 4, 36, 32, 24,
       48, 88, 44
Red: 15, 5, 10, 45, 25, 30,
       55, 50, 65
Green: 14, 21, 49, 7, 91, 42,
        77, 63

Activity 47
1. 6   6. a. baby
2. 29   b. paid
3. 19   c. dean
4. 1   d. toad
5. 3

Activity 48
1. 19 – 12   6. 3 + 1 + 4
2. 8 + 4 + 8 7. 17 – 6
3. 21 – 12   8. 3 + 6 + 9
4. 4 + 6 + 5 9. 12 – 8
5. 7 + 3 + 3 10. 9 + 7

Activity 49
1. 12   11. 12
2. 20   12. 20
3. 12   13. 20
4. 20   14. 12
5. 12   15. 20
6. 20   16. 20
7. 12   17. 20
8. 12   18. 12
9. 12   19. 12
10. 20   20. 20

Activity 50
1. 7
2. 9
3. 5
4. 48

Activity 51

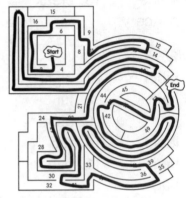

Activity 52

1.
		=	6
=	5	+	1	–
6			7
–		5	
4	=	2	+

3.
4	+	4		5
=		=		=
6		8		1
–		–		–
10		2	=	6

2.
	=	7	+
	13		6
8	–		=	3
=			–
5	+	4	=	9

4.
7	=	4	–	11
=				=
4	+	3		8
				+
17	–	14	=	3

Activity 53
1. 3 straight lines + 2 black
   dots = 40¢
2. 4 straight lines +
   1 empty circle + 1 black
   dot = 65¢
3. 7 straight lines +
   2 empty circles + 2 black
   dots = $1.20
4. 5 straight lines +
   2 empty circles + 2 black
   dots = $1.00
5. 12 straight lines = $1.20
6. 8 straight lines +
   2 empty circles + 1 black
   dot = $1.25

Answer Key (cont.)

Activity 54
1. 21
2. 63
3. 24
4. 36
5. 36

Activity 55
1. 7
2. 1
3. 5
4. 7
5. 8
6. 4

Activity 56

1.

5	3	2	1	4
2	25	4	25	5
1	5	3	4	2
3	24	1	22	3
4	2	5	3	1

2.

4	2	1	5	3
3	22	2	24	5
5	2	3	1	4
1	25	4	24	2
2	3	5	4	1

Activity 57
Across
1. 5, five
2. 3, three
4. 7, seven
5. 1, one
8. 16, sixteen
9. 10, ten
11. 44, forty-four
13. 20, twenty
15. 4, four
17. 13, thirteen

Activity 57 (cont.)
Down
1. 4, four
2. 2, two
3. 8, eight
4. 7, seven
6. 9, nine
7. 50, fifty
10. 12, twelve
12. 14, fourteen
14. 9, nine
16. 6, six

Activity 58
The following boxes should be colored:
$6 + 8 + 9 = 23$
$(3 \times 2) + 9 = 15$
$20 - 3 - 6 = 11$
$4 + 8 + 3 = 15$
$20 \div 5 = 4$
$8 + 3 + 7 = 18$
$9 + 11 + 5 = 25$
$11 + 11 + 4 = 26$
$30 - 2 - 2 = 26$
$(10 \times 2) + 10 = 30$
$3 \times 2 \times 2 = 12$
$(3 \times 6) - 2 = 16$
$(10 \div 2) + 11 = 16$
$28 - 3 - 3 = 22$
$(10 \times 10) + 10 = 110$

Activity 59
1. 4,517
2. 8,147
3. 13,066
4. 6,734
5. 11,974
6. 7,692
7. 18,557
8. 2,735
9. 4,751
10. 11,870
11. 13,095

The Great Train Robbery

Activity 60
Square #1

x →		
10	2	20
4	6	24
40	12	480

Square #2

x →		
9	3	27
4	1	4
36	3	108

Square #3

x →		
2	7	14
6	5	30
12	35	420

Square #4

x →		
6	1	6
11	3	33
66	3	198

Square #5

x →		
15	4	60
3	5	15
45	20	900

Activity 61
1. $3 \times 2 \times 8 = 48$
2. $7 \times 3 \times 2 = 42$
3. $2 \times 2 \times 6 = 24$
4. $8 \times 5 \times 3 = 120$
5. $5 \times 5 \times 4 = 100$
6. $6 \times 4 \times 3 = 72$ or $9 \times 4 \times 2 = 72$
7. $4 \times 5 \times 9 = 180$
8. $2 \times 9 \times 6 = 108$
9. $3 \times 6 \times 9 = 162$

ANSWER KEY (cont.)

Activity 62
E = yellow, 5
F = blue, 4
G = red, 8

Activity 63
1. C,4
2. B,3
3. G,2
4. E,3
5. G,5
6. G,4
7. Mount Isle
8. Emu Wharf
9. Street Beach
10. Pitt Town
11. Point Change
12. Freeway Ocean

Activity 64
1. I
2. E
3. B
4. G
5. C
6. F
7. A
8. H
9. J
10. D

Activity 65
1. 29
2. 541

Activity 66
Answer: I wanted to own a bakery, but I couldn't raise the dough.

Activity 67
Square #1

÷		
100	**20**	5
25	5	**5**
4	**4**	1

Square #2

÷		
64	**16**	4
8	4	**2**
8	**4**	2

Square #3

÷		
30	**6**	5
10	2	**5**
3	**3**	1

Square #4

÷		
16	**8**	2
4	2	**2**
4	**4**	1

Square #5

÷		
120	**40**	3
60	20	**3**
2	**2**	1

Activity 68
1. 33
2. 1,794 r1
3. 1,130 r4
4. 1,406 r3
5. 52 r4
6. 204 r3
7. 133 r2
8. 96 r8
9. 3,023 r1
10. 129
11. 1,537
12. 123 r2

Answer: Martians who landed in the garden said, "Take me to your weeder."

Activity 69
1. 36
2. 52
3. 1 1/2
4. 8
5. 5
6. product
7. 9
8. 21
9. octagon
10. quotient
11. 25
12. 100
13. 20
14. 15
15. area
16. 3,500

Activity 70
A = red, 6
B = white, 2
C = orange, 8
D = green, 3
E = blue, 7
F = purple, 5

Activity 71
1. bread
2. sheep
3. snake
4. mouse
5. apple
6. shake
7. please
8. dear
9. home
10. sleep

Activity 72
Group C

Activity 73
ADD, aid, lid, lit, nit, nut, net, new, now, tow, too, ZOO

Activity 74
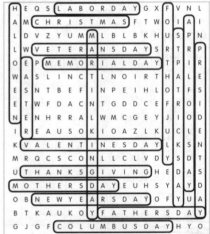

Activity 75
The notebook in the bottom right corner is Katy's.

Activity 76

1. horse
2. donkey
3. zebra
4. mouse
5. goat
6. tiger
7. sparrow
8. robin
9. eagle
10. swallow
11. penguin
12. kookaburra

Activity 77

Activity 78

1. 26 letters in the alphabet
2. 52 weeks in a year
3. Thomas Edison invented the light bulb
4. a 4-leaf clover means good luck
5. 52 cards in a deck of cards
6. 4 quarters in a dollar
7. 3 sides on a triangle, but 4 sides on a square
8. 7 continents on planet Earth
9. an insect has 6 legs, but a spider has 8 legs
10. at 32 degrees, water freezes
11. George Washington was the first president
12. 360 degrees in a circle
13. 64 squares on a chessboard
14. 4 strings on a violin, but 6 strings on a guitar
15. a unicycle has 1 wheel, but a bicycle has 2 wheels

Activity 79

1. moth, eel, zebra
2. cow, dog, rabbit
3. owl, hyena, gerbil
4. cow, owl, swan, mouse
5. flea, camel, lobster
6. monkey, zebra, llama

Activity 80

1. telephone
2. champion
3. gasoline
4. veterinarian or veteran
5. bicycle
6. airplane
7. tuxedo
8. mathematics
9. referee
10. automatic or automobile
11. refrigerator
12. submarine
13. gymnasium
14. taxicab
15. hamburger
16. spectacles or specifications
17. limousine
18. examination

Activity 81

1. Bartlett; not a type of apple
2. nephew; not a female family member
3. August; does not have a holiday; no *r* in name
4. calculus; not a type of cloud
5. oxygen; not a shape name
6. ounce; not a metric measurement
7. orange; not a primary color
8. sum; not related to multiplication
9. dogwood; not the name of a flower
10. turtle; does not hop

Activity 82

Check drawings for accuracy.

Activity 83

1. FRSTTORDEATRAN
2. FRSTTRDEATRAON
3. AFRSTTRDEATRON
4. AFRTTRDEATRSON
5. ANRTTRDEATRSON
6. ANDRTTREATRSON
7. ANDRREARSON
8. ANDRREJARSON
9. ANDRERJARSON
10. ANDREJARSON
11. ANDREJACKSON
12. ANDREWJACKSON

Activity 84

1. Turkey
2. Iran
3. Canada
4. New Zealand
5. France
6. Israel
7. Poland
8. Wales
9. Peru

Activity 85

1. waterfall
2. broken leg
3. made in China
4. multivitamins
5. vacation overseas
6. bad speller
7. double vision
8. Tennessee
9. backwards

ANSWER KEY (cont.)

Activity 86

Activity 87

10 triangles

25 rectangles

Activity 88

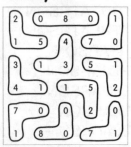

Activity 89

Check drawings for accuracy.

Activity 90

1. I'm hot
2. I go for it
3. Black Velvet
4. Lovin' You
5. You're nosey
6. Burn rubber
7. Your plate here
8. Ladybug
9. Our Secret
10. Antique Lover
11. Baseball Star or Basketball Star
12. I'm too busy

Activity 91

1. Teacher
2. Lawyer
3. President
4. Doctor

Activity 92

1. cold
2. colt
3. bolt
4. bold
5. bald
6. ball
7. bell
8. belt
9. melt
10. molt
11. mold
12. mole
13. hole
14. hold
15. gold
16. fold
17. food
18. fool
19. tool
20. pool

Activity 93

Across	Down
2. out	1. gas
4. cake	3. uptake
6. draw	5. ends
8. beaver	7. trigger
10. colors	8. bee
	9. log

Activity 94

1. A stitch in time saves nine.
2. A bird in the hand is worth two in the bush.

Activity 95

1. F, after
2. T
3. F, odd
4. F, west
5. T
6. T
7. T
8. F, third
9. T
10. F, Washington D.C.
11. F, penny
12. T
13. T
14. T
15. F, 9
16. F, does not
17. T
18. F, thirteenth

Activity 96

1. volcano
2. South Pole
3. earthquake
4. France
5. oceans
6. Hawaii
7. Australia
8. mountains
9. jungle
10. lake
11. California
12. equator

Activity 96 (cont.)

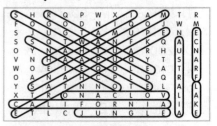

Activity 97

1. a secret or silence
2. rug or carpet
3. a towel
4. your breath
5. a shadow or reflection
6. a dictionary
7. egg yolk
8. a hole
9. a river
10. a tissue or paper

Activity 98

1. Gerald Ford
2. Ronald Reagan
3. Andrew Jackson
4. George Washington
5. John Adams
6. Abraham Lincoln
7. John Tyler

Activity 99

Answers will vary.

Activity 100

1. archery
2. wrestling
3. rowing
4. gymnastics
5. fencing
6. luge
7. equestrian
8. cycling
9. skating

Answer: Athens, Greece

Activity 101

1. penguin
2. cabbage
3. Hungary
4. Turkish